IN THIS TOGETHER

IN THIS TOGETHER

FIFTEEN STORIES OF TRUTH & RECONCILIATION

Edited by
DANIELLE METCALFE-CHENAIL

Brindle & Glass Publishing
An imprint of TouchWood Editions
103-1075 Pendergast Street
Victoria, BC V8V 4E4
Brindleandglass.com

Cover and interior design by Pete Kohut

Library and Archives Canada Cataloguing in Publication
In this together : fifteen stories of truth and reconciliation /
Danielle Metcalfe-Chenail.

Issued in print and electronic formats.
ISBN 978-1-927366-44-8

1. Native peoples—Canada—History. 2. Native peoples—Canada—
Social conditions. 3. Native peoples—Canada—Government relations.
4. Reconciliation—Social aspects—Canada. 5. Canada—Race relations.
I. Metcalfe-Chenail, Danielle, editor

E78.C2I422 2016 971.004'97 C2015-907638-2

We acknowledge the financial support of the Government of Canada through the Canada
Book Fund and the Canada Council for the Arts, and of the province of British Columbia
through the British Columbia Arts Council and the Book Publishing Tax Credit.

The interior pages of this book have been printed on 100% post-consumer
recycled paper, processed chlorine free, and printed with vegetable-based inks.

Printed in Canada at Friesens

16 17 18 19 20   5 4 3 2 1

. . .

For all our relations

CONTENTS

1   Introduction | DANIELLE METCALFE-CHENAIL

11   The Importance of Rivers | CARLEIGH BAKER

23   Dropped, Not Thrown | JOANNA STREETLY

35   Drawing Lines | ERIKA LUCKERT

45   Jawbreakers | DONNA KANE

53   This Many-Storied Land | KAMALA TODD

67   The Perfect Tool | ZACHARIAS KUNUK

75   To Kill an Indian | STEVEN COOPER *with* TWYLA CAMPBELL

87   Two-Step | KATHERIN EDWARDS

99   Echo | CAROL SHABEN

111   Mother Tongues | KATHERINE PALMER GORDON

123   White Aboriginal Woman | RHONDA KRONYK

133   Colonialism Lived | EMMA LAROCQUE

145   Marking the Page | LORRI NEILSEN GLENN

159   Lost Fires Still Burn | CARISSA HALTON

171   From Aha to AHO! | ANTOINE MOUNTAIN

183   A Conversation between Shelagh Rogers and
the Honourable Justice Murray Sinclair

209   Contributors

INTRODUCTION

DANIELLE METCALFE-CHENAIL

T HERE WERE TWENTY-FIVE of us chatting on folding grey chairs in the program room at an Edmonton, Alberta, public library. We fell silent when Miranda Jimmy, a young Cree organizer and community leader, called the meeting to order. Miranda, wearing glasses and an intricate turquoise clip at the top of her long, dark braid, invited us to stand. We joined hands in a circle as she recited a secular prayer: that we find inner strength and comfort in the group; that we take care of ourselves; that we ask for what we need—a moment, a tissue, a hug. As we went around that circle introducing ourselves, I realized we were made up of a range of ages, backgrounds, ethnicities, and genders. There were City representatives, parents, artists, writers, educators, students, and community workers.

Miranda told us how she recently recognized she needed to start sharing her experiences of intergenerational trauma brought about by the residential school system with the wider Canadian society. For the past decade, she had shared with other survivors, but she worried that the energy generated by the Truth and Reconciliation Commission (TRC) and Edmonton's Year of Reconciliation would fizzle. She was worried the TRC would be all political rhetoric and no real change.

Most of her Aboriginal friends were cautiously waiting to see what came of the first meeting, she said, and as we introduced ourselves, only three people self-identified as Indigenous. Her friends were frustrated with repeated failed attempts at communicating their concerns and sick of being "consulted," she added. I saw nods from the group. A métis woman in the circle who worked for the City echoed their sentiments: "I'm feeling cynical right now," she said, her shoulders slumped forward.

There were a lot of other feelings identified that evening as we went around the circle. One non-Indigenous person said they felt ashamed of the past. Another, a relatively recent immigrant to Canada, said the enormity of the issue of reconciliation was overwhelming. Many mentioned wanting to "do things right" through proper protocol and a sensitive approach; not knowing where to turn to figure this out, they found themselves paralyzed.

One of the other participants, a métis poet called Anna Marie Sewell, prompted, "Just begin."

This collection of essays is only one of many ways to begin the work of reconciliation in our country. We recognize that we don't hold all the answers in these pages, but in the contributors' "aha" or light bulb moments around our country's colonial past and present, we hope to seriously (and at times humorously) question the status quo. The authors included in this anthology are journalists, writers, scholars, visual artists, filmmakers, a former city planner, and a lawyer. They are Indigenous and non-Indigenous individuals from Tofino to Igloolik to Halifax. In these pieces they investigate their ancestors' roles in creating the country we live in today, and how we might move forward together in respectful partnership. They look at their own assumptions and experiences under a microscope in hopes that you will do the same.

This project was born out of a phone conversation between Brindle & Glass associate publisher Taryn Boyd and me in late March 2014. We had never spoken before then, but we quickly realized we had a lot in common as lapsed academics interested in Canada's colonial history. At the time, the TRC events were concluding in Edmonton and our conversation kept circling around how to keep discussions going in mainstream Canada. Finally, in an aha moment of her own, Taryn suggested we work on this collection. I was excited. And terrified of doing it wrong.

Just begin.

As a white, middle-class woman and as a student, writer, and now Edmonton's Historian Laureate, I've wrestled with a lot of the same questions as the contributors. And, as is the case for many of the essays you'll read here, it hasn't just been one big aha moment for me, but a series of light bulbs going off:

1. It's 1991 and I'm nine years old watching TV in our Ottawa home. There are soldiers and police in full riot gear facing off against men in camouflage. There are guns. I hear that it's in a place called Oka (Kanehsetake) near Montréal, Québec, where a lot of my father's family lives. I remember thinking, *Why are these people so mad at each other? How can this be happening in Canada?*

2. In middle school I do projects on "les Iroquois" but it's all longhouses and corn—no golf courses or Sacred Pines in sight. My mother does contract work for the federal government and I make pocket money as a teen helping her sort news clippings that come by the box-load. I scan and highlight the articles, sorting them into piles, while I listen to my Discman. In this way I learn about Davis Inlet and the Innu in Labrador, kids in their teens like me who are living in abject poverty, huffing gas, dying in house fires, and killing themselves in suicide pacts. I try to understand the situation and share it with my Grade 13 classmates in our Families in Canadian Society class.

3. There are rumours in the family that one of our ancestors is Indigenous but "passed for white"—Régina Lagesse or "la sauvagesse," as some called her. I can't understand why someone would be ashamed of being Aboriginal and hide it from the world.

Like many non-Indigenous people who "wake up" to this reality in our country, at first I looked at it in very simplistic terms: black and white, victim and victor, oppressor and oppressed. As a natural defender of the underdog, I came face to face quite suddenly with feelings of "white guilt" and wanted to do something to fix the situation. Luckily, I had fantastic teachers along the way at McGill University and the University of British Columbia who saved me from my own good intentions and taught me about the complexities of colonialism. I learned about agency and how power works, and about race and gender and class and how they intersect. Some of it was through really theoretical texts I'm still not sure I understand, but some was through powerful personal narratives. These stories embodied the theories—literally theory made flesh—and made it all real to me.

We wanted to capture that realness in this collection of essays. When I read Emma LaRocque's experiences of public school as a Métis child, I feel the sting of her teacher's backhand. I am with Joanna Streetly in her kayak below the cliff face, wondering if the boy at the top will topple a boulder and kill us. I am paddling the Yukon's Peel River with Carleigh Baker, wrestling with hunger and sleep deprivation and the ghost of my grandmother. When Erika Luckert is on the floor carving out a map of Treaty 6 territory, I am sitting beside her, watching her work. When Antoine Mountain heals himself through art and faith, I am transported as well.

We also wanted to capture the rollercoaster ride of thoughts and emotions that come with this journey of learning our collective past and our personal identities. Rhonda Kronyk is a living example of how government laws and policies, along with corporate actions, can erase family histories and dictate what you're allowed to call yourself today. Donna Kane unpacks her family's identity as homesteaders and her younger self's feeling that things would be better "if only we could all be the same." Katherin Edwards and Carol Shaben both come face to face with some of their unexamined assumptions and find uneasy friendships in the process. Lorri Neilsen Glenn shows how closely connected we are through genetics, that the missing and murdered Aboriginal women we hear about are "all our relations." Or, as Carissa Halton was told by one of her Indigenous colleagues, Cheryl Whiskeyjack, as she looked at shifts in Edmonton's child welfare system: We are all treaty.

Many of the contributors throw down the gauntlet and challenge us to examine our prejudices and stereotypes around Indigenous peoples in Canada. Steven Cooper and Twyla Campbell ask us to look at the histories we've been taught with a critical eye, and to hold ourselves as a nation accountable for past wrongdoings. They don't want us to wallow in settler guilt but to have open discussions that acknowledge all sides, and change curricula and textbooks to reflect a more accurate and inclusive version of the past. They don't want us to stall in "truth telling" mode, either, though. These writers encourage us to push for real reconciliation in concrete forms. Kamala Todd wants us to remember that all cities are, at their core, Indigenous territories that we need to learn about and honour through place making. Katherine Palmer Gordon shows us in stark relief how critical Indigenous languages are to the lives of individuals and communities. They tell us to create government programs that work in real partnership with

Indigenous communities, and, as Zacharias Kunuk says, recognize the cultural importance and traditional knowledge of Indigenous peoples on anything from snowy owls to the Franklin Expedition.

These contributors have opened up their hearts, minds, and lives in these pages for our collective education. We all believe that when we know better, we do better. Part of this education for me has included learning about indigenizing writing, editing, and publishing. As you read the essays, you'll not only notice different writing styles, but also worldviews and narrative approaches. A couple of the pieces flow heavily from oral cultural expression and don't necessarily fit Western modes of written storytelling. I hope you will appreciate these distinct voices and recognize that part of the decolonization process is making space for different ways of knowing and being.

I have tried to standardize some terminology across the essays, using the currently preferred terms "Indigenous" and "Aboriginal" except when authors have specifically chosen a different word or phrase that is meaningful to them or can refer to a specific nation. I also have used the broadly inclusive "small m" for "métis" when talking about individuals of mixed European and Indigenous ancestry and reserved "capital m" "Métis" for the descendants of the Red River Colony as laid out in the Constitution Act of 1982. While some might see this concern with words as simply about political correctness, it goes much deeper than that: words have power and create our understandings of the world. Part of reconciliation is recognizing the immense variations in cultural and political makeup of different Indigenous peoples in Canada, and how identity has been so tied to colonialism. These realities are reflected in the words we use, so we should choose them wisely.

I heard someone say on CBC Radio recently that anger without hope is a destructive force. In these essays, as well as in that Edmonton library room in May 2015, there are certainly instances of justified anger and frustration. In this region in the last year alone, we have heard about a downtown mall kicking a respected local Elder out while he was eating noodle soup, and a twenty-nine-year-old NDP candidate facing racial slurs when she was campaigning for a provincial seat. But we have also had outpourings of support for those individuals, a mayor who has declared that sacred ceremonial space will be created within city limits, and a sold out Walrus Talks on the Aboriginal City that saw 1200 people pack the Shaw Centre. Now, from a small group in a library, RISE (Reconciliation in Solidarity Edmonton) is hoping to build a broad coalition and make change happen. The first project? A heart garden where we could make change—one conversation, one message, one heart at a time. And as we closed the circle of our first meeting with handshakes and hugs, there was a sense of hope even as we recognized the enormous challenges ahead.

•   •   •

Thanks to associate publisher Taryn Boyd, editor Renée Layberry, and the folks at Brindle & Glass for being so keen on this idea and bringing this collection of essays to fruition, and to Erinne Sevigny for connecting me to Taryn in the first place. Thanks also to the Edmonton Arts Council for supporting the project with an Individual Artists Grant. A huge thank you to all the contributors to this collection who squeezed their writing into already jam-packed schedules, and to Shelagh Rogers and the Honourable Justice Murray Sinclair, who taught me an incredible amount about these interlocked questions along the way. I appreciate their patience and generosity. Thanks also to my wonderful husband and young son who challenge me to think about and communicate these ideas in new ways, and to my extended family for walking, talking, and posting about reconciliation right alongside me. *Merci. Miigwetch. Mahsi Cho.* We are all in this together.

THE IMPORTANCE OF RIVERS

CARLEIGH BAKER

I N SEPTEMBER 2014, I paddled 500 kilometres through the Peel River Watershed in the Yukon, as part of a documentary about art, adventure, and Canadian identity. The film also had environmental implications, as the Peel region is currently under threat of gas and mining exploitation. On July 7, the Supreme Court of the Yukon began hearing the case filed against the Yukon government by First Nations, the Canadian Parks and Wilderness Association, and the Yukon Conservation Society. The Supreme Court ruled in favour of the people, but as of March 2015, the government is in the process of appealing that ruling. The six artists on the trip were invited to address the environmental concerns however they wished, or not at all.

In essence, this was a documentary about the artists, six urbanites with varying degrees of outdoor experience, on the Peel River for nearly a month. The film would document what we'd learned from our time in the northern Yukon and Northwest Territories landscape, and interpret its link to our identity as Canadians. There were also two scientists on the trip, two guides, and, of course, the film crew—twelve of us in total. At thirty-seven, I was one of the oldest on the team. Most of the participants were in their mid-twenties. Everyone on the crew was non-Aboriginal, except me, a mixed-blood with little knowledge of my Métis heritage. Which is where paddling 500 kilometres across the Canadian North comes in.

When I was asked to be part of the Peel Project documentary, I thought of my Grandma Carrière right away. A lack of pride in her French/Cree background kept her from being a part of her family and her community. As I get older, I've wanted to fill in the space that remained after her death. I thought the time spent on the Peel considering our relationship might bring about some epiphanies. I didn't know exactly how. But this is what people do when they want to find themselves; it is the classic transformative journey story—go, suffer, find out who you are. This was my call to action, so I agreed. I packed a photo of Grandma Carrière into a dry bag, along with journals, pens, rain gear, and a hundred layers of merino wool long johns. I suffered. I paddled. I did not find exactly what I was looking for.

. . .

Holy crap, I'm hungry.

The GPS says we passed the Arctic Circle. Time to celebrate, or at least feel like superstars for a few minutes, though our river journey still isn't over. My fellow intrepid travellers haul out their otherwise useless iPhones and we take photos of one another: Oh my god, me in the Arctic! Facebook-ready for whenever we get anywhere near a signal. Fort McPherson? Maybe Dawson City. We'll be ready.

It's not a postcard moment: the weather is misty and grey, the river big and brown and sluggish. Earlier in the trip things were more scenic, but now it's muddy shores, scrubby trees, and, beyond that, bare-ass mountains. We've been paddling through the Peel River Watershed for sixteen days, and we've got about four to go. I'm tired and cold and dirty, but I hope Grandma Carrière would be proud if she could see me now, flush-faced and grinning, posing for a picture with a canoe paddle in hand. "Bravo, Chérie," she'd say, using the accent that only really came out when she was drunk and swanning around like Edith Piaf. Yep, my Métis grandma was a boozer, and this prevented me from getting to know her very well when she was alive. Her habit may have robbed me of a grandma, but it also robbed me of the opportunity to learn about how to be a part of the Aboriginal community, and my Métis extended family. Fortunately, it's never too late for the latter.

A little farther down the river something extraordinary happens. We hear a boat, the only motorized sound we've heard since the trip began, besides the fancy drone camera the director uses for "money shots." Our canoes all rafted together to share a snack, we listen to the boat's approach, and excitement starts to bubble. Outside contact! Soon, a long flat-bottom boat appears. Three people are in the front, bundled up in parkas, and one is working the outboard motor in the back. They pull up beside us; greetings and names are exchanged. Ernest and Alice Vittrekwa are husband and wife and Margaret is Alice's younger sister. Kirk is on the outboard; he's in his late teens or early twenties and introduced as an adopted son.

Alice seems to be a few years younger than Ernest, who isn't easy to understand since he's missing teeth and he mumbles. He says something to us and Alice repeats it. "A little late in the season for canoe trips."

Somebody answers that we're making a movie about the Peel, and the three adults nod approvingly. Everyone who lives on the Peel is savvy to the situation and invested in its protection. In some ways we're only well-intentioned enviro-tourists, but those who make the Peel their home understand that everyone's help is valuable. Ernest is right though—it *is* late in the season. The Whitehorse companies who outfitted us for the trip said the same thing, politely implying that we are nuts to be travelling in September. Our connections at the Canadian Parks and Wilderness Association insisted on regular check-in calls with the satellite phone, even though our guide is local and very experienced.

We laugh about this, and eventually someone cracks a joke about how we've been pushing to finish the trip before we run out of food. It's funny because it's true. There's giddy laughter, but a question now hangs in the air between the Vittrekwas and us.

"Well, you better head over to our camp," Ernest says, answering it. "It's just down a ways."

Alice and Margaret aren't smiling, but they nod. Twelve people—
that's a lot of unexpected guests. "There's a kettle, there's coffee
and sugar," Alice says. "Get some coffee on. We're going a little
farther up to look for moose." And so we are unceremoniously
dismissed, left to paddle the last few kilometres to a stranger's
camp, in search of coffee and a warm fire.

*   *   *

The Aboriginal people of this land have been providing aid to
underprepared dumbasses like us for hundreds of years now,
especially in the inhospitable North. Helping those in need is an
ingrained part of northern Aboriginal culture, just as not asking
for help is considered rude or wrong-minded. And we could use
the help. The food situation has been grim. There have been
whispered conversations about reducing portion sizes, already
pretty skimpy for long days on the river. Lunches are the worst.
On day two of a gruelling portage, we were given a tortilla with a
smear of cold refried beans, a sixth of a can of tuna and shredded
cheese. I took extra beans and looked around, daring somebody
to object. It's making me nervous, and it's having an effect on
the group dynamic too. Things are getting . . . well . . . weird.
Gaunt, pale-faced travellers loom over whoever is cooking dinner
and watch like so many wolves when portions are ladled out.
At breakfast, people comment on how many apricots I have in
my bowl, or how slow I'm eating. I eat slowly because it creates
a feeling of fullness, but the number of calories remains the
same—inadequate. Everybody has to have a say on when snacks
are portioned out, and it only takes one naysayer, inexplicably

proud of their capacity for self-denial, to delay a stop for lunch or a snack break for an hour, even though the very suggestion of food has already started my salivary glands working, stomach growling. This decision-making by committee is driving me crazy, making me angry and resentful of anyone who doesn't want what I want, when I want it. The Vittrekwas' invitation, once extended, sends a current through my cold, worn-out body.

．　．　．

A few kilometres down the river, their camp appears on our left. We pull our canoes up onto the muddy beach and make for higher ground. There's an outhouse and a smallish shack with a bowed roof. Across from that is a lean-to, where I find the hearth. A battered aluminum kettle on top of the grate. Some dried meat, moose, somebody guesses, and dried fish. Under a tarp is a big table set up with coffee and sugar, as Alice promised, but also butter and jam and evaporated milk, all kinds of delights we haven't enjoyed for what seems like an age. A little farther off is the main house, small and cozy-looking, with a rough deck out front. There is nothing fancy here, nothing ornamental. It looks, to the privileged eye, like poverty. I think about Grandma Carrière's shelves jammed with porcelain dog figurines, and the gold-threaded Mexican blankets draped over rattan couches. She lived in Coquitlam, British Columbia, a long way from her Red River heritage. With her blue-rinse perm and her polyester pantsuits, she clearly preferred the Florida pensioner aesthetic to that of the Métis voyageur. She liked rivers though—or at least she felt at home on the river. In the photo I brought on the trip, she's walking along the Alouette River shoreline in Maple Ridge, BC. Three dachshunds, her stalwart companions, are by her side. She is wearing a pantsuit—mint green—the beaded moccasins on her feet likely the product of some kind of eighties Native American fashion trend. She's smiling her beautiful smile, eyes squinty behind thick glasses. The Alouette is the river my dad spread her ashes in after she died. Rolled up his pant legs and waded in while those of us on the shore sang "Amazing Grace," for lack of anything better.

While she was alive, Grandma Carrière's devotion to alcohol made her a loner. She continued to drink heavily, even after most of her family had gone sober. My dad was her only child, and our communication with her remained sporadic, often contingent on her sobriety. But after she died, the family communication lines opened somewhat. A reception at the Maple Ridge Ramada followed the spreading of her ashes, and a bunch of the Métis family I had never met was there; we sat around a table and made awkward conversation. No significant tears had been shed, and the memories people shared were distant and disjointed. Building a clear picture of who my grandma was wasn't easy. Eventually, two of her sisters-in-law cornered me over a cup of coffee and then tried to act nonchalant when they asked what I remembered most about her.

"Her wiener dogs," I said, and laughed. And then I realized what a stupid, shallow answer that was. "I, uh, didn't know her very well."

Their faces opened to me. "She was hard to get to know," one said. We all nodded. We talked about my grandma's youth and they hinted at familial skeletons: abuse, Catholic shame, neglect. They couldn't say where exactly the shame came from that caused my grandmother to drink and to try to erase both her French and Cree backgrounds. And I may never know, since family secrets, personal bias, and the decline of memory wind history into knots.

"She was always so angry," another woman said, one of Grandma Carrière's blood sisters. All three nodded. "She was the angriest of us."

.   .   .

There's a tentative-looking husky tied up near the bow-roofed shack, cowering a little but wagging his tail. As good as coffee sounds, animal affection wins the day, and I approach fearlessly, burying myself in him and nearly bursting into tears at the contact. The dog pants and lets me hang around his neck like a yoke. I can hear the Vittrekwas' boat approaching.

Despite the invite, our team was unwilling to make themselves at home in the Vittrekwas' absence. But swept up in the current of our hosts, things just happen. The fire gets made and coffee is brewed in giant pots. Cups are distributed, and I fill mine before anyone else. People make jokes about how much I've missed my coffee, since we ran out days ago. Alice leads a few of us into the smaller shack, where a wood stove creates a three-dimensional heat none of us have experienced for weeks. They say we can sleep here for the night and the thought is intoxicating. Food is produced at such a rate we can barely keep up. Cookies and biscuits, bannock with butter and jam, dried fish and candies and, of course, endless coffee.

At one point, Alice pulls me aside. "Why didn't you pack enough food?" she asks, eyes narrowed.

"You're asking the wrong person," I start, raising my voice to implicate some of the people who were actually in charge of food, but I can see she's genuinely concerned, and now's not the time for humour.

"Why didn't you call ahead, ask us for help?" By "us" she means everyone at Fort McPherson, the band office, and a whole town full of experts in northern travel that would have been happy to offer guidance.

"I don't know, Alice. I was told there would be enough, and I trusted the people in charge."

"What do any of you know about being up here?" she says, huffy and frustrated and a little bit sad. Classic grandmother.

I start to offer excuses, the same excuses I'd been feeding myself for the last several days as I grew hungrier and hungrier. "Nothing," I say finally. "Certainly not enough. We should have asked for help."

She nods, vindicated, lower lip protruding. And then she goes back to making sure everyone is fed. After dark, wieners are produced for us to roast, mustard passed around. She finds me again, the fire dancing across both of our faces, a piece of buttered bannock still locked tightly in my grip. We talk about home and family. Or mostly, she talks and I listen. The Elders are smarter than you. I may be an ignorant mixed-blood, but I know this. So shut up and listen, and don't fill the quiet spaces with your words. And if you can roll with this, and let them have their space and adequate time to fill it, the benefits to you, the listener, are immense.

I'm reticent to tell her I'm Métis, nervous it might lead to questions I won't know how to answer. But I can't resist mentioning Grandma Carrière.

"So where is your family?" she asks.

"Well, my Métis family is from Manitoba," I say, "Red River settlement. But my family lives in BC."

"They're a long way from home then."

"You're right, but it was never really our home. My Grandma Carrière moved out west with her family when she was a girl," I said. "I don't know much about it."

"Why would she leave her home?" Alice's lower lip is jutting out again.

"My grandmother wasn't very proud of who she was," I say, "She drank a lot, so we didn't see her very often anyway."

This, Alice understands. She nods. "It's not your fault," she says simply, immediately.

I nod and gulp, feeling like I might cry. Alice's eyes are watery, but she nods with determination.

"It's not your fault," she says again. This is not ancient Elder wisdom. This is Al-Anon, straight from the blue book. Fort McPherson is a dry community, but that doesn't mean there's no drinking. A little knot is tied between the two of us, Alice and me. We've found a common language, at least for tonight: the language of healing.

I've never thought much about how Grandma Carrière's drinking affected me, but who doesn't walk away from a relationship with an alcoholic wondering what they should have done differently? I was an adult when she died; there was nothing stopping me from forging a relationship with her while she was still alive. I didn't want to. I think about how it affected my dad, having to cut off his own mother from contact for months, sometimes years at a time, the ultimatum of her sobriety hanging between them like an anvil. My mom, angry because I'd answered the phone when Grandma called and had been subjected to one of her drunken rants. The rage that swept through the house after my mom seized the phone from me on one of Grandma's drunk dials, with her asking my mother what her IQ score was. My mom, from an immigrant family in which she and her brother are the only two with university degrees.

And really, that's what I remember most about Grandma Carrière. Not her anger, but the anger that surrounded her. My selfish, sulky anger at the lack of grandmothers in my life who baked cookies and took me to the park to feed the ducks. Why the hell didn't I have one of those?

Now I'm angry. But this is what Alice was talking about; this is the part that's not my fault. It's not my fault that I didn't want to get to know Grandma Carrière while she was alive. That I'm more likely to rewrite her now that she's dead, with significant edits. And it's not my fault that she's not here with me in spirit on the Peel, though I wanted her to be. People like her are never there for you.

I take these thoughts to bed with me, so I don't sleep much. Most people don't sleep much in the warm cabin, twelve of us packed in head to head like so many sardines. I don't think most people care; they're enjoying every minute of a full belly and the all-encompassing heat. The stove crackles and clangs, people gurgle and burp and fart like nobody's business, the chests of those able to grab a few z's rise and fall in a soft rhythm.

The next morning, we take our time packing up and cleaning the shack, savouring every last moment indoors.

"Looks like you had a good chat with Alice," one of the other artists says to me.

"I did," I say, not sure how to fill in the blanks for him. Very little was actually said. That's how these things work sometimes.

For breakfast, it's oatmeal and boiled eggs and dried fish, and the Vittrekwas send us off with more than enough supplies to keep us fed and caffeinated until the end of the trip. I am thankful but sheepish. Even with the best of intentions, we have continued in the colonial tradition of underprepared tourist/adventurers, and benefited from the Aboriginal tradition of offering help without expectation. Well, maybe one expectation.

"Just make sure you tell people about the Peel," Alice says, waving away our repeated thanks. "Good luck," she says to me, when I hug her goodbye. I'll have plenty to tell people about the Peel, and about Alice. Maybe less to say about Grandma Carrière. If anything, I feel like I have more questions than answers now. That sounds clichéd, but no more so than the idea of finding myself on the river. It takes a lot more than a canoe trip to get in touch with your roots. And it will take more than a team of well-intentioned, accidental colonials to save the Peel. But it won't be wasted effort. As the people of the Peel know, everyone's help is valuable. That's how community works.

DROPPED, NOT THROWN

JOANNA STREETLY

I WAS NINETEEN WHEN I moved to Tofino, on the west
coast of Vancouver Island, to work as a sea kayak and whale-
watching guide. That summer, I fell in love with a person and
a place, both at the same time.

The place I fell in love with was Clayoquot Sound, a collection of inlets and islands on the west coast of Vancouver Island,
named after the Tla-o-qui-aht people. These seafaring people
were masters of the dugout canoe, travelling great distances up
and down the coast. They were unafraid to hunt the whales that

could, once harpooned, tow the hunters miles offshore, out of sight of land. Like many coastal people, the Tla-o-qui-aht were seasonal nomads, following the salmon from the mountainous upper Clayoquot River, down through the inlets, past Meares Island, and out to sea, as far as Long Beach.

The person I fell in love with was a Tla-o-qui-aht canoe carver, who co-owned the whale watching boat I was working on. By summer's end, I had abandoned my plans to leave Tofino, overwhelmed by an unexpectedly deep sense of belonging.

At that time, my knowledge of Indigenous cultures was limited to the arrowheads and clay pipes my brother and I had found as children growing up in Trinidad—an island in the Caribbean whose gentle native Arawaks had been completely wiped out within two decades of Christopher Columbus's arrival in 1498. Caribs from Venezuela took the Arawaks' place, but met a similar fate with the result that full-blooded Amerindians no longer exist in Trinidad. This had given me the sense that Indigenous people were a historical concept, and several subsequent years in England only served to reinforce that.

And so, when I arrived in Canada, my notion of First Nations people was limited to the carvings of Bill Reid and the contents of the Museum of Anthropology at the University of British Columbia. I had no context for an actual living, breathing, present-day culture.

1990 gave me a crash course.

Night after night I lay awake, examining the slant of my partner's cheekbones and the heaviness of his long black hair. I wondered who I was and how we had come to be together.

I dreamed vividly about whales and water and other worlds. I became untethered from my own self, immersed in a new universe.

By contrast, my partner had a strongly defined sense of self. He knew what he stood for and what he wouldn't stand for. He told me of injustices endured by First Nations people at the hands of European settlers and church representatives. I learned how this injustice had carried through to the present day.

1990 was the summer of the Oka crisis. Even without my new perspective on life, the notion of building a golf course on a burial ground seemed deliberately provocative. *Golf*, of all frivolous things! Ancestral remains were an issue in Clayoquot Sound, too. Burial caves had been looted by non-Native old-timers, claiming an interest in history. Burial islands had become the domain of summer homes, small cabins cropping up amid the ancient spruce trees, in whose high branches were lodged the remains of ancestors, preserved in moss-draped wooden boxes.

Tofino at the time was a hot-button place, having lived through the heated environmental protests of Meares Island and Sulphur Passage. The logging of Meares Island was prevented through a concerted effort by First Nations and environmentalists; thus in many ways these two groups—with a mixed array of aims, from preservation to land rights—wound up on one side of a fence, while the logging fraternity squared up along the other.

Add to this restless mix a long history of Saturday night fights between Natives and non-Natives outside the Maquinna bar and you have the basis for the kind of explosive behaviour of September 8, 1990, at the intersection of First and Campbell Streets in Tofino.

On that day in September, what started out as an information protest about the army at Oka, and the stoning of Mohawk women and children there, erupted into a geyser of aggression. The protest was planned as a peaceful affair but turned into a volatile mess of beer-drinking hecklers shouting racist epithets, and hyper-charged people in trucks trying to ram the protestors, about 75 percent of whom were non-Native. Two children narrowly escaped being run over. Innocent tourists were threatened. Communication was reduced to "Fuck you, fucking asshole!" Even Old Ben, one of my favourite Elders, is forever etched in my mind's eye, waving his stick above his head and yelling to the hecklers in his frail voice, "Why don't you come over here and tell me that?"

What shocked me was the rapidity with which the situation ignited. My small town had flown from peace to war in five minutes. The aggression was supported by a self-righteous anger that had no clear foundation and yet it was there, simmering under the surface in a way I hadn't perceived. I saw with sudden clarity what my partner meant when he told of the prejudice he and his family had faced in their lives. And the words of Hesquiaht chief Simon Lucas—who had spoken beautifully at the close of the protest—echoed through my head:

"You only see us with one eye."

. . .

Following that summer, I settled into a shared life for the first time. Our small apartment filled with things my partner and I had made together—a table, shelves, small carvings. I learned to drive a boat and help with the winter beachcombing of logs. I dug clams, picked oysters, and ate duck soup, fish-head soup, herring roe, and many other traditional foods. I began to learn Tla-o-qui-aht words, kept a dictionary, listened to the soft nuances of the language.

At around this time I was reading *The Songlines*, by Bruce Chatwin. In it, he told of Australian aborigines, for whom the world is not alive until they have walked through time—along dream tracks dating back to creation—singing each landmark into existence along the way. I identified with the aborigines. I, too, was awakening to a new world, its features coming alive for me as I did so.

I attended potlatches and visited my father-in-law's house for regular dinners. Slowly, I began to meet the large group of people who made up my new family. And without exception they were friendly, welcoming, kind. When spring arrived I felt like a changed person. But who was I? I didn't know yet.

And then I experienced a different kind of baptism.

* * *

When they came, the deaths were brutal, shocking, relentless.

A beautiful eleven-year-old niece was accidentally shot by a boy firing a semi-automatic pellet gun at random into the bushes, near the village of Opitsaht. Hit in the shoulder, she was dead by the time she reached the boat that was to take her to Tofino.

Up until that moment, my exposure to death included the natural demise of an elderly grandmother and a high-school acquaintance killed in a car crash. I grappled with the ending of this young life, wondering how my new sister-in-law could ever survive it. I cried in the street and on the phone to my mother in England. I cried when I saw other people who knew about the accident, and I cried when I had to tell people about it. I couldn't believe that this girl was dead. Life had gleamed in her eyes and her grin. Life had danced in her quick limbs.

It couldn't be.

My dreams changed. They became vivid, troubled. One morning I awoke to an image of slaughter, a heap of animals dead on the rocks at an island. What woke me was the phone ringing. Another message of death—this time the suicide of a nephew.

Again, I failed to make sense of it. This young man had just graduated high school, had won a car for his popularity. This young man, whose life was just taking flight, had deliberately planned its end. Again, I wondered how his mother would survive—how his sisters and brothers would cope. We stayed in Port Alberni, sweating through a heat wave, crying and talking at a rectangular table in a small square kitchen. The calm dignity and wisdom of my bereaved sister-in-law stayed with her in her grief. I took comfort from her, aware of the irony in that.

And then there was another nephew, this one stabbed. Still so innocent, I didn't understand the mercurial urgency of running to the hospital in the middle of the night. In my mind's eye, I saw a paring knife stuck in a leg, requiring just a few stitches. I simply didn't anticipate what a large kitchen knife could do to a chest: the hospital floor, so sticky with blood, darkening as it lost its purpose. I gazed at his once-loving, once-laughing face, taking in every detail of skin, hair, tooth. Twenty years later, this lifeless face still gazes back at me, reminding me of what can be lost—and how quickly.

I hadn't been prepared for another death, so soon and so violent. I felt reborn, but not in the positive sense of that phrase. For me, the passage was from light into darkness, the darkness of things that shouldn't be. If I had been searching for a song-line of my own, by now I was returning to the comfort of Mozart's *Requiem*.

By this time I had also learned that grief could be a community affair. No hushed whispers or darkened doors. No leaving people alone or giving them space for reasons of privacy. Here, one's presence in a grieving household was considered a mark of respect. Human company was known to be the best possible medicine. Visitors came from all over to sit with the grievers in living rooms packed with rows of chairs.

I became proficient in the culture of death, the protocols required. When word of a death reached our ears, we went to the Co-op and filled bags with essentials: coffee, bread, cheese, ham, and mayonnaise. Hundreds of people would pass through the grieving household, requiring nourishment. And then there were the coffins. For a family facing an unexpected death, or several deaths in a row, the cost of a coffin is crippling. Even in winter, when work was scarce, we would empty our pockets and hand over what we had: crumpled fives, tens—sometimes even coins. Rent seemed trivial compared with the need for a coffin. Time, also, seemed irrelevant on these occasions. One's own plans became unimportant, replaced by the need to help wash dishes, pass out food, or simply sit in silent solidarity with the gathered crowd.

The deaths continued apace. A rash of suicides culminated with that of an eight-year-old boy. In what was another first for me, a young man died of AIDS. A young woman vanished without a trace, last seen at a party, still lost even now.

My mother came to anticipate phone calls that began with "Oh Mum, it's so awful . . ." She provided much-needed transatlantic sympathy. She never commented on the constancy of the stream of events. Sometimes I wondered if she understood how bleak I felt, how hopeless.

I began to see the Native community as a people in perpetual crisis. There never seemed to be time to heal from one event before the next one struck. The paralysis of grief affected everyone. Death cast long shadows, in the shade of which it was impossible to function. By comparison, John Jewitt, a blacksmith from the ship *Boston* who had been a slave of the Mowachaht tribe 200 years prior, remarked on the robust health of the people, their strength, toughness, and the astonishing paucity of deaths. In the three years that he spent with them, from 1803 to 1805, only five people died out of 1,500. I read his diary with a bitter sense of wonder. So much had changed.

. . .

While I was stuck in my new-found state of bewilderment, Tofino was changing. In 1993, close to a thousand people were arrested in defence of Clayoquot Sound. Multinational logging corporation MacMillan Bloedel fell to its knees, while tourists from around the world arrived to see the place that had attracted such international media attention.

That same year, I travelled to Haida Gwaii to work as a kayak guide at the southern tip of Gwaii Hanaas National Park. I was excited to see the totem poles and village sites that this dramatic, storm-tossed coastline was so famous for. And yet, as I paddled through the islands, never meeting a soul outside of our group, I experienced a deep sense of loneliness. Everywhere we went there should have been people—thriving communities vibrant with families, art, life. The blacksmith Jewitt could have met these people, admired them the way he admired the Mowachaht.

When death struck Gwaii Hanaas in the smallpox epidemic of 1862, it left only silence. The few surviving southern souls—only 30 percent of their original number—moved to the north to amalgamate with other tribes. All that remained of their presence were rectangular shapes in the mossy forest floor where houses had once stood. Even the magnificent totem poles had fallen or broken off and were crumbling in front of my eyes. I touched the mossy house poles, trying to imagine their inhabitants alive and vital. I mourned the loss of these families and saw for the first time the magnitude—the colossal, shocking decimation—that was contact.

My innocent potted history gleaned from the UBC Museum of Anthropology was transformed by a visceral sense of comprehension. On their own, museum displays simply can't convey the reality of cultural decimation. Perhaps this is what is wrong with race relations in Canada. Too few people can *feel* what happened. No song-lines exist to describe it. No voices remain to sing it.

By now, I saw the world with a built-in set of contrasts—the world I'd grown up in and the world I was only just beginning to know. I also saw two communities rapidly diverging.

Tourism spawned a housing boom in Tofino. In the equivalent of an old-fashioned gold rush, land mongers, developers, and speculators rushed onto the peninsula. Land was no longer a place of story and connection. Many buyers were strangers, separated from our small community by their wealth and newness. By contrast, the Native community, so entrenched in family and historical connection, was collecting for coffins.

The contrast was illustrated one day when a friend of mine finished work at the school. One of her Native students had cried because she had no money for her school portrait. Moments later, her husband came home telling of a landowner who was choosing a front door for a brand new house. The choices ranged in price from $5000 to $10,000.

The cultural divide was already conspicuous. The wealth gap was making it more so—resentment in the making. Taking a minor key, my song became one of unease.

In summer, the waters of Clayoquot Sound are packed with visitors. Surfers, whale watchers, sports fishers, kayakers. Like migratory birds, they flock to the traditional territories of the Tla-o-qui-aht, the Ahousaht, and the Hesquiaht. Yet few First Nations have any contact with these people. For the most part the visitors are faceless, meaningless, perhaps a source of income, perhaps just a source of annoyance. And the day I became a faceless, meaningless tourist will stick with me forever.

It was a beautiful evening. I was out for a sunset paddle in my kayak. Gliding out of the harbour on the ebbing tide I passed close to Grice Point, the bluff where tides are measured. Up on the bluff a group of Native boys was partying. I could tell by their whooping cries that they were high—very high.

And then they noticed my kayak and jeered over the edge at me.

"Throw a rock," one of them shouted. And quick as winking, a boy heaved a boulder into his arms, grunting at the effort.

By now I was truly worried, sweat pooling against my tightly gripped paddle, thoughts of my young daughter swirling with the eddies. To these boys, I was faceless, just as they—daily—were faceless to non-Native people in Tofino. Two communities living side by side, unknown to each other.

My voice carried strongly up the bluff as I recognized one of the boys and called out his name. There was a silent pause and the other boys turned to face him.

"How come she knows your name?"

I never heard the reply because they moved away from the edge. Instead, I heard the dull thud of the rock as it fell to the ground—dropped, not thrown.

Saved. I'd been saved by a name.

* * *

My partner and I separated after seven years. His life continued to be wracked by tragedies—the loss of a grandson, the loss of a daughter, the loss of his father. With his father went the family home and I no longer had a place to visit in Opitsaht. Deprived of my usual way into the community, I saw with sudden clarity that initiating cross-cultural friendships can be complicated. Hypersensitivity to racism on either side breeds awkwardness, mistrust.

But at the same time, the lack of such relationships in our town is shocking to me. Indifference prevails. I feel as if I have to lead by example—take more time when I see people in the street, address them by name, reinforce my interest in their lives. The burden of indifference weighs heavily on me.

. . .

For the Australian aborigines, a *tjuringa* is a sacred stone, engraved with the part of a song-line that belongs to you. In recent years I've retraced the steps of my song-line, going backwards to find my way forward. I haven't yet found the perfect words to engrave, but what stands out is the importance of names.

Names are the only way we have of showing recognition. It is difficult to crush someone with a rock if you know their name. Likewise, it is harder to diminish people—treat them as lesser or treat them with disrespect—if you know their name, their circumstances, their lovable traits, their weaknesses.

If the Native and non-Native communities are to cross the gulf that separates them, in Tofino and elsewhere, we have to begin with individual relationships, the recognition of people as people. And as we say each other's names, so we sing them alive, awakening our own selves along the way.

DRAWING LINES

ERIKA LUCKERT

I GREW UP IN Edmonton, Alberta, and for all of my childhood and most of my adolescence I had no idea I was living on treaty land. In fact, if you'd told me I was living on treaty land, I wouldn't have even known what that meant. When I did start hearing about Treaty 6, it was in passing, as a courtesy and little else. At the beginning of an event: "We'd like to acknowledge that we are on Treaty 6 land." (*Now on to more important things*). It wasn't until I finally sat down and read the treaty that I began to consider its incredible importance.

The document itself doesn't look like much, but I was struck by how few words it took to cede such a large swath of land. Treaty 6 covers more than 190,000 square kilometres in the midsection of what are now Alberta and Saskatchewan, including the cities of Edmonton, Lloydminster, Saskatoon, and Prince Albert. And all it took, in 1876, to write that land away was a single paragraph. The treaty describes the boundary in terms of the land's natural features, taking rivers and mountain ranges as its markers to draw a line from Cumberland Lake in Saskatchewan, through Alberta to the Rocky Mountains, and back through the southern part of the two provinces. *Thence westerly up the said river to its source, thence on a straight line in a westerly direction*—the dated phrases sounded almost poetic to my modern ear. *To the junction therewith of the outlet of said river.*

I had to force myself to read past the elegant prose to its effect. Traditional lands stripped away with a few sentences. All of the people who lived on those lands, with this treaty, would *cede, release, surrender and yield up* that home, *forever*. Yes, those are the words they used. And there wasn't even a map—nothing to show how large this land really was, how important. Nothing to hint at the magnitude of what was being surrendered that summer of 1876.

Well over a hundred years later, reading this treaty, I wanted to understand those things. I wanted to understand just how these words defined the land, to understand this treaty the only way that I, as a writer, knew how. I wanted to follow its words. So I set out mapping them. I took the text from the treaty, and I found a map of the treaty boundary. I began with the first words of that colonizing paragraph—*commencing at the mouth of the river*—and I wrote the words in their place on the map. *Commencing.* I wrote the words all around the boundary line, repeating them like an incantation until they reached the places on the map that they were trying to claim. *Thence up the said river, against the stream, thence up the said river, against the stream, thence up the said river, against the stream, to the Jaspar House.* And when the boundary wrapped its way back around, *following on the boundaries of the tracts conceded by several treaties numbered four and five, to the place of the beginning,* I took the boundary line away so that only the words remained. The words *were* the boundary. It was the words that cut the land away. They hung there on the page like a loose lasso, a string of words that, on such a scale, looked more like a rope that you might use to tie someone up and drag them away.

Plotting the map with those words, I discovered something of their power, their violence. But I discovered something else, too, as I tried to follow the official boundary line. That line was wrong. In places, the official boundary simply did not accord with the treaty text. The boundary did not follow the words, or the words did not follow the boundary. There were places where the words got stuck, where the line turned too sharply for the letters to follow, or where the boundary was not in the place the words described at all. I later found that another scholar had seen the same thing, and was attempting to recreate the boundaries in strict adherence to the original treaty descriptions, following the rivers that it took as points of reference. But I wondered, still, how accurate those revised maps would be. After all, haven't the riverbanks been worn over the years? Haven't the rivers' beds shifted? Haven't layers of soil been washed away, and others built up higher? Hasn't the earth been turned and ploughed and poured full of asphalt, highways, the concrete cores of cities? Is the land that was ceded way back then the same land that I live on today? And is accuracy really the point, anyway?

A few months after my experimentations with the Treaty 6 map, I was at the Provincial Archives of Alberta, poring over stacks of yellowed notebooks. From 1871 to 1917, around the same time that the country was being parcelled up and sold, treaty by treaty, the Dominion of Canada sent surveyors to map the land, and to divide it into a legible grid of townships, ranges, and sections. The surveyors kept notebooks in which they recorded details of the landscape, foliage, and soil, all the while bisecting it with neatly ruled lines. There are hundreds of these notebooks. I read only five or ten, but what I glimpsed was astounding.

The books betrayed their age—they were bound in brown paper, the pages yellowing, their spines starting to crumble. Each was signed by the surveyor who had written it, and each, though written by different hands, was filled with elegant script, the fading ink and careful penmanship signalling another time. On each page, there were perfectly drawn shrubs, rivers, trees, and delicate annotations. In places, the words even followed the lines of the land, curving along its contours—*country undulating, thickly wooded with poplar, spruce*, or *mostly open prairie, with occasional patches of poplar and willow brush*. Just as when I first read Treaty 6, my instinct was to read it as poetry. The words, and the lands they charted, were beautiful. But then I struck upon a line that reminded me what I was really reading. *The soil is all of first-class quality and although scrub is plentiful, the land will not be difficult to break.*

These notebooks were not journals of an appreciation for the land; they were plans for the appropriation of it. As the surveyors carefully noted each shrub and soil type, they drove stakes into the ground, marking out the corners for fields, farms, roads. Their task was not to embrace the curves of the land, but to break it into squares. They were dividing the entire country into range and township lines, into a massive grid that would make it easier to map, and to control. They were claiming the land.

When I drive across the Alberta prairies today, I follow the same lines that they marked back in the late 1800s. Range and township roads cut across the province, and the country, in a metred grid. *The land will not be difficult to break.*

That, in so few words, is the story of settler Canada. Land, broken by range and township lines, by treaties and ceded countryside. Land broken by the desire to own, to possess. And all of this is caught up in mapping. A scholar called John Pickles once wrote: "The world has literally been made, domesticated, and ordered by drawing lines." By making maps. Maps have been a powerful tool of colonialism, not least because we take them to be true. Who would question a map? How can we dispute the location of a town, the path of a stream? In truth, though, a map is more like a story. And those who make the map determine the story that will be told.

When we begin a map, or a story, we select scale, detail, context. We choose what to conceal, what to reveal. It is said that writers draw on personal experience—well, every map is personal too. It's a projection of the personal. In mapping, a projection refers to the way the world is skewed to make it visible on the page. The Mercator Projection is the view we recognize from school textbooks; it's the same view we carry in our pockets daily, on our smartphones, with Google Maps. But it misses things. Greenland is not actually larger than China. Europe is a mere fraction of the bloated landmass it appears to be. In the Mercator Projection, you can never see the poles of the earth, because the map's distortion makes them extend to infinity.

Any way you go about it, we're flattening something that isn't flat. In fact, it isn't even spherical. The earth is an oblate spheroid, and not even a perfect one at that—it's covered in hills and valleys, in jagged edges that are always shifting. Lewis Carroll knew the impossibility of making a perfect map. One of his comical characters, Mein Herr, announces with pride, "We actually made a map of the country, on the scale of a mile to the mile!" When asked if the map has proved useful, he confesses that it hasn't even been unfolded, for to spread it out would cover the entire country and block out the sun. But the clever characters find another solution: "We now use the country itself as its own map, and I assure you it does nearly as well."

When we try to pin a country to the page, we change it. It's just like, for example, writing this essay. I get to select the details, the parts you will and won't read. I can choose to conceal the fact that I am white, middle-class, and have never suffered the consequences of Canada's colonial history. Or I can drop that information onto the page in an offhanded way, in an attempt to make you think less about my privilege, to make me think less about it. Every map does this too—it exercises certain privileges, usually without revealing them.

Of course, mapping is not only a colonial practice—maps of Canada existed long before the Europeans arrived to chart it. A few summers ago, I found myself at a cartography conference, attending a presentation about Aboriginal mapping. It was entirely re-orienting. We were shown an Aboriginal map of a mountainous area, alongside an equivalent, more conventional map of the same place. It was impossible to rectify the differences between the two until I abandoned one of our most fundamental cartographic assumptions. North was not up. And nor was east, or west, or south. The map took the mountain peaks as its point of orientation, so the relative distances were distorted in relation to the jagged range. The map's representation was attuned to the landscape in a way I could never have conceived.

And then I learned about another type of map that wasn't on a page at all. Rather, it took a piece of the landscape as its canvas. These were maps made of wood, carved along the length of a sturdy stick. A map not of a place in its entirety, but of a single journey through the place—the path paddled along a river with all its turns and tributaries was carved into the wood so that paddlers could follow the map with their fingertips, all the while looking downstream.

I started to wonder if maps, just as they conceal parts of Canada's Aboriginal past, could also help to reveal it. If a map is just a means of representation, could it not also represent those parts of the land, and of its Indigenous heritage, that have been broken? While maps can certainly limit the understanding of a place, closing our view to focus on a single dimension—a boundary line, for instance—they could also open up parts of a landscape that can't be seen.

Edmonton, the city where I grew up, is built around the bend of a river and is the longest continually inhabited place along the North Saskatchewan. Long before the Hudson's Bay Company came up the river and built Fort Edmonton, there were Aboriginal encampments there. Archaeological remains have been found, and mapped, from 7000 years ago, near the place where a decommissioned power plant sits today.

I wanted a way to imagine these histories without so much city in the way, a way of conceiving the land beneath it all, before Edmonton was built. I wanted to see my city in a way that was impossible without the aid of a page: without houses, without streets, without sidewalks or even trees. I wanted to see the land, alone, and to read its lines. And so I mapped it. I created contour maps, where each line is a level of relief, where each curve carves the page into a landscape of new depth.

These days, when cartographers want to look at the contours of an area of land, they create 3D graphical models, but I didn't want that level of technological sophistication. It felt distanced, disconnected from the earth. Instead, I took the elevation data I had downloaded, and I flattened it, leaving contour lines where hills and valleys used to be. The lines swirled across my computer screen, meandering along the river, and twisting off into hills and swells. I didn't label them. Instead, I printed those lines, and began the process of bringing them closer to the land they represented.

I took my printed map and heated up an iron. As if the copied map wasn't smooth enough, I held the iron over it, pressing it flatter still, until the ink transferred onto a sheet of linoleum below. Then, with the city so thoroughly flattened before me, I began to carve. I cut away the lines, dug into the linoleum landscape to leave valleys in the ironed map. I peeled away pieces of the landscape and watched them accumulate like the tailings at the mouth of an underground mine. My fingers ached from the effort of cutting away each contour, and I thought of the forces that had made the landscape I was depicting: rivers, floods, footsteps, time.

With the carving finished, I made the map flat again, to render it legible. I rolled ink over its plane and pressed it onto a fresh page, imprinting an image of a landscape that I have never once seen in all my years of walking this city. It looked like water, rippling in lines across the page, or a tangle of yarn, waiting to be unwound. It looked like a story, like a language that I might learn to read.

.   .   .

Years ago, on a trip to the Rocky Mountains, I stayed in a rustic cabin filled with equally rustic books. One was an old school textbook from the late 1800s, called *Peter Parley's Universal History*. It's an incredibly biased, inaccurate text, entirely of its time, that goes so far as to classify the people of the world as savages, barbarians, semi-civilized, and highly civilized. "American Indians," unsurprisingly, are classed among the savages and are described as having skin "the colour of a dead leaf." *Peter Parley's Universal History* is racist, colonial, and altogether distasteful, but it does get one thing right: it acknowledges the limitation of a map. *We must be content with maps and learn geography from them as well as we can*, it says.

A better way to learn geography, according to Peter Parley, would be to travel the world in a balloon. *If you should enter a balloon, rise into the air, and sail along over the country, how many interesting things would you see!* But even that picture would be incomplete. What of the sod or grass houses that would seem mere hills when viewed from above? What of the burial sites and the places of prayer and the narrow paths of animals through the trees? We must *not* be content with maps. We must challenge their limitations, open their representations, and re-imagine them in ways that makes them tools not of colonialism, but of reclamation.

The young student who first owned that copy of *Peter Parley's Universal History* had drawn all over the book's maps, colouring inside their lines, and outside too. It was doubtless the act of a distracted child during a dull lesson, but it makes me think, none-theless, of the necessity of writing back to the colonial landscape, of rewriting our established ways of mapping it. I wasn't able to begin to think about the meaning of this country's Aboriginal legacy, and the land that I live on, until I began drawing my own lines. When you start making the map yourself, you start to ques-tion it—you have to question it. And that seems to me a good place to start.

JAWBREAKERS

DONNA KANE

Y FATHER ARRIVED in the Peace River country in 1931. He was three months old. There is a photo of him being propped up by his older sister, Doreen, on the steps of the log cabin built by my grandparents on land we still call "the home quarter." By the time my father was a young man, he had homesteaded several of his own quarters and married my mother who'd come from Prince George to teach in a one-room school. Together they had three daughters, of which I was the second.

My dad spent many years cutting down aspens and willows,

jack pines and spruce, pulling the roots out with his tractor, pushing the fallen trees into brush piles to burn before turning the charred earth with a plow, loosening the clods of gumbo until it became a field. Each spring, a new crop of rocks and leftover roots would be unearthed, and we would pick them. My dad "broke" the land, but he also loved it. Whenever he had the chance, he was out checking birds' nests, deciphering animal tracks, searching the beaches and shallows of the Kiskatinaw River for fossils, finding ammonites, small coiled sea creatures extinct for seventy million years. The land we crossed to reach the Kiskatinaw River was also owned by my parents, and there was a hollow, a dip in the middle of a field seeded with timothy grass where a seasonal creek threaded its silty way. Whenever the creek dried up, my father would look for arrowheads—exotic black stones with a lacquer finish, edges nicked into a triangular shape.

As a child, the surface of the rock reminded me of the round licorice jawbreakers we'd buy at Ted's Service on Sunday drives. It took forever to suck the hard ball down to its centre. As each sugared band dissolved in my mouth, it exposed a new flavour. At the core was hot cinnamon. It was what I looked forward to, working my way through the other flavours to set my tongue on fire.

I don't know how my father viewed the arrowheads, but at the very least, he would have seen them as collectible; I saw them as part of the natural world. If I thought of the people who carved them, they appeared in my mind as shadowy sepia figures, emerging then dissolving back into the land. Fossils and arrowheads were the same to me—evidence of life once here but no longer.

Mine was not a multicultural community (our one ethnic restaurant was Chinese—of the sweet and sour chicken balls variety). We were pioneers who may have come from different countries—the United Kingdom, Ukraine, Poland, Scotland, Ireland—but our general culture and beliefs were more or less the same. We celebrated Christmas and Easter, we were Protestant or Catholic, we ate meals consisting of meat, potatoes, and vegetables. I never thought of myself as a colonialist. We were settlers, pioneers—generous, hardworking folks trying to make a go of it. I do remember my dad saying that the land we lived on had perhaps been used for hunting by Aboriginal people (as evidenced by the arrowheads), but they had never settled here; they were always just passing through.

Growing up, Amy was the only Aboriginal person I knew, though no one would have used the word "Aboriginal." Many would have called her a Native or an Indian, and the derogatory connotations of those words at that time would have been intended. My parents encouraged us to never judge anyone, so they weren't words I used. I thought of Amy as a foster kid, someone who slept in a house that wasn't her own. For a brief period of time when we were both around thirteen, we rode the same bus to school. Amy sat at the back, and I sat one seat ahead. She was filled with a restless energy, shifting her body on the green Naugahyde bench, looking for ways to liven things up. She was nice if a little terrifying. Sometimes she'd light a cigarette, then take a few drags before grinding the lit end on the heel of her boot. My fear would be as sharp as the smell of sulphur from the struck match, more afraid of being somehow implicated than of Amy being caught.

Wherever Amy came from, it couldn't have been from here. Here was where the pioneers had come to stake their claim on land to prove it up. My family was the first to settle the home quarter. Wasn't that proof that we were the ones who'd really lived here, that the Aboriginals, who were just passing through, were less rooted to this landscape than we were? And I really was rooted to my place. As a kid, I knew the path to the river like the movements of my body; the grasses and flowers and trees felt a part of my flesh and bone. I knew the river's clay banks, the places where cliff swallows built their crockery nests beneath the overhangs, the beaches where geese would lay their eggs then lose their flight feathers. I knew the smell of sun baking the clay into honeycomb cracks and the scent of rain splitting the grains of earth apart, the clay absorbing the moisture back in, expanding luxuriously, mending the fissures. I'd sleep outside on a mossy bank in a copse of pine trees beside game trails formed by bear, moose, and coyote. I was selfish. I didn't want anyone to know my place better than I did. I kept my history small. Maybe land had been stolen; maybe there were reserves and residential schools, but not in Bessborough, not on this block of land renamed after a British lord. And the Kiskatinaw River? That the word was Cree for "cutbank" was something I'd read in a book by explorer and geologist George Dawson. I liked the way the translation made the word "Kiskatinaw" more concrete, making clear the river I knew so well, how the water cut its way through the clay, creating steeper and steeper banks. But I didn't stop thinking of the word "Kiskatinaw" as mine. Cree remained an abstract. The word and the people it referred to were not real to me in any experiential way. The Kiskatinaw River was.

I was thirty before I finally acknowledged I was descended from colonialists. I was working at the local college while at the same time attending first year university transfer courses: psychology, English, sociology. On the day of my light bulb moment, my sociology professor stood in the doorway of the office where I did my clerical work. We were discussing the lecture he'd given on Aboriginals, and at some point I heard myself say, "If only we could all be the same." And he said, "The same as who?" I felt myself grow hot as Kiskatinaw clay in the sun—shrinking then splitting apart. Why had it taken so long for the realization to come, and why had it come at this particular moment?

No doubt the change had been coming for some time, but slowly. Like the layers of the jawbreaker, my assumptions had been wearing away, one sugared band at a time, but when the truth revealed itself, it still came as a shock. Those four words, "the same as who," exposed a core belief I'd been blind to until that moment: I realized I thought of myself as the cultural norm, the inevitable outcome of any human on earth removed of barriers. Barriers that, if asked, I couldn't have named. By "same" I meant "just like me." My colonialist beliefs and traditions were as deeply imbedded in me as the landscape I loved. And that wasn't all. Not only had I seen the way I lived as normal, I saw it as ideal, what everyone would aspire to if only they had the chance. I never saw the foster homes and Americanized Chinese food as evidence of the opposite—clear examples of what happens when we disturb someone else's culture, when we try to force people to assimilate, to make us all "the same." I'd never imagined how I would have felt if I had been forced to leave my wood-frame home and live in a teepee, made to speak Cree, to bead and make bannock. As rich and fulfilling as these activities are, it wasn't my culture. The culture I was born into carried a history I could trace from my parents to their parents and so on, a culture that had been passed from generation to generation, layer after rich layer, our family tree recorded inside recipe books and wedding albums. I was a part of something continuous, the changes so slow they appeared seamless.

Clearing trees, upturning the earth, and turning the land into fields were just the beginning of what we'd broken. Children like Amy, descended from families severed from their culture, were not dissimilar to the roots we picked each spring. There may not have been evidence of Aboriginal camps when I was a child, but that doesn't mean they weren't once there. And that they aren't there today, alive and well, teaching, creating community gatherings, and sitting on City Council.

It took me far too long to realize the assumptions I'd made. It's embarrassing, the story a cliché. But today, twenty years later, I still hear people—kind, intelligent beings—saying the same thing as I once did: that all of our problems would be solved if everyone were treated the same. "The same as who?" I'll say, hoping to make the same impact as my professor. Sometimes the answer will be, "You know what I mean." Sometimes it will be, "I am not responsible for my ancestors. They were the colonialists, not me." Some will use their ancestors as an example of how colonialism was never the problem. "After all," they will say, "our ancestors had to move from their homeland and look at how well they did." In all of these comments, colonial thinking remains. At the core of asking why we can't all be the same, of why Aboriginal people can't just accept things as they are, is a searing belief that fails to recognize that our ancestors were allowed to bring their cultural traditions and spiritual beliefs with them. In the home country of the Aboriginals, the government worked hard to try to rid the Aboriginal people not just of their land, but of their cultural being.

Getting to the core of our colonial beliefs takes time, and the truth at the centre can be hard to digest. In recognizing the flaws of my thinking, I have also had to come to terms with the fact that, along with the hard work and perseverance of my ancestors, there was, at best, an ignorance and, at worst, a disregard for those who came before us.

For me, the layers of assumptions and practices that blocked the recognition of my colonial past were inextricably bound up in emotion. It wasn't just the guilt for what colonization did to Aboriginal people—it was the sense that, in acknowledging the actions of my ancestors, I was somehow betraying the people I love, people who worked hard to make my life better.

For years, my dad would bring home the arrowheads he found. On rainy afternoons, sitting in the living room, he'd show them to me. I can almost see the drawer he kept them in, but the house is sold now, and no one knows what became of the lustred rocks that once reminded me of those jawbreaker candies.

Like my father, I too have searched for arrowheads and ammonites. I've never found an arrowhead, but I have brought ammonites home. I still have one on a shelf in my office. But most of the fossils I've found were composed of sediment similar to the river's clay. Once removed from the water, they split and crumble apart. But the clay in the Peace River country is also resilient. It is able to reconstitute itself. Like the rain that binds the clay-gumbo back together, the Aboriginal people in my community have shown that, despite the concerted efforts of colonialism, we have not been able to destroy their culture, and people like me are recognizing the fissures in our thinking.

And by admitting those flaws, I feel oddly liberated. Like my pioneer ancestors, I want to be the best person I can be, but I now realize that I have a better chance of achieving that goal not by always being right, but by recognizing when I'm wrong. As more information on residential schools and other colonial attempts at assimilation are revealed, I am given an opportunity that many of my ancestors did not have—a clearer picture and better understanding of the unforeseen impacts that the pioneer life, like any kind of life, has had on others.

Writing this essay has been a tremendous help in my own struggles with settler guilt. By thinking deeply and writing down the ways in which I once thought about Aboriginal culture, I have become more aware of how I think about all cultures. This has helped me appreciate my own life more fully.

I will work on my reconciliation for the rest of my life. I now walk through each day with a greater awareness of how my actions and thinking may impact others—and with the hope that, over time, I can better meld my responsibilities as a settler with the richness that was also a part of my family's history.

THIS MANY-STORIED LAND

KAMALA TODD

OW WELL DO we know where we live, if our ancestors are elsewhere? What do we have to go on? For many of us, it's the surface of our urban environments, the diverse pathways and spaces of our everyday lives. Certainly, we all form relationships with our place, based upon our complex network of interactions with it. But, I ask again, how *well* do we know the land where we live? Not just the familiar spaces of work, commerce, leisure, and home, but the meanings, the offerings, the laws of the land, the depth of human, plant, and animal continuity upon these now concretized landscapes. How deep is our understanding?

I'm a Métis-Cree transplant in Coast Salish territory—what is now called Vancouver, British Columbia. I have a very strong relationship with this land. My cells have been nurtured by sea, moss, cedar breath, salmonberry. This is the only land I truly know. My mother arrived here from the Prairies as a young teenager and had me soon after. My own children were born here and are growing up in this beautiful rainforested place. My father, a child of German immigrants, was also born here. This is undisputedly my home. But I have no illusions about being *from* here, in that deep, Indigenous sense. This is not my land. My ancestors come from Cree grasslands, Ireland, and Germany. My roots here, though strong, are very new.

To live in someone else's traditional territory is to build new roots and homes, but not necessarily understanding. If we are not Indigenous to our place, we may be oblivious to just how deep the roots go, and how destructive city building has been to the land and to the people who have always lived there. We may have a very shallow knowledge of where we stand. While every North American city is what I call an Indigenous City, most of these cities conceal their Indigenous roots. Despite sharing the land and wealth upon which the city was built, despite providing the know-how and labour to build the city, Indigenous people have been largely excluded from place making. How did it come to be that thousands of years of Indigenous presence are ignored? What are the consequences of this invisibility?

HOME

I grew up in a pretty Native world, with meetings at the Friendship Centre, powwows, adopted aunties from many Nations. My mother was active in the Aboriginal community, and so I was mindful of the struggle for equality and self-determination. But the world around me told a different story. According to my schooling, any sort of Native civilization was a thing of the past. Of course I knew better. I knew that this is all Native land—all of the Americas. But I still had a very limited understanding of the Coast Salish nature of my city. I knew this Vancouver I lived in as a West Coast place of cedar, masks, and longhouses. But I knew very little about the place names, languages, traditional cultural landscapes, protocols of the land where I lived. It wasn't until my early twenties that I began to deeply understand the layers of Indigenous history everywhere I step—and how the making of Vancouver has impacted Coast Salish people.

THE LAND IS THE LANGUAGE

Much of my deeper understanding came from relationships with local leaders, Elders, artists, and friends. While studying at the University of British Columbia, I learned more about the Musqueam people and their tireless work to exercise their Aboriginal rights and title, to be heard on their own land. When my mother, a gifted filmmaker, invited me to co-produce a story about the Tsleil-Waututh Nation and their urban treaty, I was inspired by their approach of building partnerships and "putting the face of the Tsleil-Waututh back onto the map of their traditional territory." Through these relationships and the generosity of Coast Salish people, I learned more about the extensive cultural landscapes that were here for millennia before Vancouver was built. Village sites. Gathering places. Longhouse culture. Rich stories of transformer stones and runners and watchmen, and mountain goat wool gathering in the North Shore mountains. Welcome figures, house posts. (Not totem poles, as the northern coast people make.) I learned that the language of this land is hən̓q̓əmin̓əm̓. I didn't learn any of this in school. Nor did I learn it from any official telling of Vancouver's story, or the physical landscape itself.

As I learned more of the ancient history of my city, the depth of Indigenous knowledge and cultural continuity here, I grew angry that so many people were oblivious to it. The dominant narrative is so skewed. We are left with gaps and silences, walls of denial and resentment when Indigenous people speak out or make decisions on their land. I was tired of hearing people say that Vancouver is a young city with no history. I was tired of reading tales praising the "Great White Fathers" as the founders of a 200-year-old settlement.

WRITTEN ON THE LAND

How do we transmit cultural stories and values? As I watched my mother blossom into the gifted storyteller she is, I learned the importance of voice. Her conversation with Leonard George, son of the late Chief Dan George and Amy George, was incredibly illuminating. They asked, "What are the main sources of oppression for Aboriginal people?" They listed the big ones: "Church, state, educational system." And they added one not normally seen as complicit: "Hollywood." At that moment, my mother knew that she had to take on the racist, stereotyping images that were out there. I always tell that story because it emphasizes the power relations that permeate all aspects of our everyday lives. My mother talks about the inherent right to tell our stories from within our cultures and identities. With her powerful films and writings, she takes on silencing and oppression through self-determination of voice, culture, aesthetics, and language. Her work has made me believe in the power of telling our stories, of making space for marginalized voices.

My university education inspired a way of looking at the land that was very compatible with my cultural teachings, and my sense of justice. Two degrees in urban geography taught me how to "read" my urban environment, to see the taken-for-granted urban landscape as text. Whose stories are told? Whose cultures are visible in the built form? Who controls it, defines it, defends it? Who gets to shape the layout, aesthetics, and dominant norms of how we live on this land? It was with these hypercritical eyes that I found an inscription that would help me to really identify and challenge the colonialism of my city.

I came across a simple plaque downtown on Hastings Street. One day while hanging out at the offices of *Redwire*, a local Native youth magazine, Secwepemc artist Tania Willard told me to wander down Hastings to check out a highly offensive plaque. I made my way there, already tense with anger, bursting through the clouds of smoke and music of Victory Square, tripping on the uneven cobble of Hamilton Street. (That grey stone always gets me thinking about the nearby land that was blasted to make the tiles and bricks for Vancouver's streets and fancy buildings.) I searched the nondescript low-rise bank Tania directed me to. There, in cast bronze relief, was Vancouver's archetypal origin story, commemorating the location where its first land commissioner stood in the "silent solitude of the primeval forest" and "drove a wooden stake in the earth and commenced to measure an empty land into the streets of Vancouver." I shook my head. *How can people erase entire societies—the very societies that shared this land and its abundant wealth?* There was the evidence, writ large, of how Indigenous people have been written out of the story, and how the myth of *terra nullius* has been deeply embedded. In overwriting the stories of the local Indigenous people, in depopulating the land and claiming it as free for the taking, these typical "first spike"narratives present the city as a place made and founded by the dominant Anglo culture. There is no space for Indigenous people in this story, or in this remade place. Such normalized histories reinforce the segregation and dismissal of Indigenous people on their own land. There is little to no sense of accountability to any laws, protocols or Indigenous rights and title because, after all, there was "no one" here.

Seeing this upsetting colonial fiction inscribed on the landscape, I was more determined than ever to challenge this harmful narrative of erasure. And I realized that the best way for me to do this was through story, using the tools I have as a filmmaker, and the access to municipal decision-making I have as a community planner. My mother, as a formally trained and gifted filmmaker, had taken on Hollywood; I, an urban geographer, would take on the myths and stories of my city.

To be clear, Vancouver's Indigenous history is not my history. It's not my story to tell. Like all Indigenous people, Coast Salish people have always held their stories, asserted their rights and title, kept their cultures strong. It's the wider community that needs to do the work, to listen and to learn. I knew at that moment that I wanted to help facilitate that work. I firmly believed that the more people listened to the Indigenous stories of this land, the more people learned how Vancouver was really made, the more understanding and inclusion we could achieve. I dreamed of the day when residents and visitors alike would have a clear understanding that Vancouver, like all North American cities, is an Indigenous City. A Coast Salish city.

CITYSCAPES

Fresh out of grad school, I was asked to come and work for the City of Vancouver's Social Planning Department. A phone call came out of the blue. *We need to build better relationships with the Aboriginal community.* My boss recognized serious gaps in the City's relationship with Aboriginal residents. I was reluctant at first, mistrusting of government and skeptical that any change could be made within "the system." *Thanks, but no thanks. It's just not my thing.* But my boss was a wonderful ally who knew how to make things happen, and, it turns out, Social Planning (now called Social Policy) is the "social justice" arm of the City. I had the privilege of being Aboriginal Social Planner from 2000 to 2006, and since that time, I have witnessed a gradual increase in awareness and move towards reconciliation and dialogue. But it didn't start out that way.

From my first days working at the City of Vancouver, the lack of awareness, and the lack of Aboriginal inclusion, was staggering. There were almost no Aboriginal staff. We had no Aboriginal committee, no Aboriginal Affairs office, no dedicated Aboriginal positions, no Aboriginal policy. Despite being on Coast Salish territory and having Canada's third largest Aboriginal population, despite the statistics that showed Aboriginal residents experienced a disproportionately higher degree of quality of life challenges, there was relatively little interface between the City and the Aboriginal community. When I asked about the relationship with the local First Nations, I was told, "We don't go there," because it's a federal issue, a treaty issue. We had service agreements (water, garbage, sewage) with Musqueam, since they are in the City of Vancouver area, but that was about it.

The City's website didn't even recognize the Coast Salish people. In fact, when I clicked on the link "About First Nations," I was taken to an external tourism website that claimed, "The people who used to live here were Haida." Wow. They sure had that wrong. Another time, a director of planning told me the local First Nations were a "special interest group" who didn't need to be included in a major document visioning Vancouver 100 years from now. After I suggested to planners working on a massive new community on the Fraser River that they consult with the Musqueam people—the people who have always lived on the river—I was dismayed to learn this outreach never happened. So many missed opportunities.

STORYSCAPES

Fortunately, I had an open-minded boss committed to seeing things improve. He noted that many Aboriginal residents said they felt invisible, and he was keen to address this. And so, with my belief in the power of story, I pitched him a project that would support

Aboriginal residents in sharing their stories of Vancouver. After some reflection, he agreed, and in 2003 I launched Storyscapes as a way to gather and share Aboriginal stories of Vancouver—and, hopefully, help change the narrative of brave pioneers and founding fathers in an empty land.

Storyscapes was all about connecting with people and gathering stories from diverse Aboriginal residents. We had Aboriginal youth research and conduct oral history recordings of different neighbourhoods. We had a video project in which youth interviewed their Elders and added to their community's oral history archives. We made two short films with Aboriginal residents of the Downtown Eastside (DTES)—a very misunderstood community that is continually spoken for and shaped by outsiders. One unforgettable meeting with residents of the DTES affirmed my belief in the power of story. I was there to listen to their concerns. One man, who laughed constantly and showed the wear of life on the streets, let me know how fed up he was.

"With all the so-called consultation, the grassroots residents are not being heard," he said. "It's always the same service providers at the table."

I offered the bureaucratic solution: "I can contact the planner for your area and tell him to come and meet with you."

"Nah, there's no point," he replied. "It's through these videos with you that we'll really get our voices heard." In one unforgettable meeting I had with Aboriginal residents there, one man, fed up with not being heard in the "consultation" process, told me he was hopeful about making a video, because it was "the only way we are going to get our story out there."

Storyscapes Chinatown was another memorable project. My beloved auntie, the late Gitxsan artist Doreen Jensen, used to call me at City Hall and gently guide me in areas of work.

"Someone really needs to talk about some of the shared history between Chinese and Aboriginal people," she told me one day. "There's important stories there." Several community leaders had been telling me about the little-known history of Chinese and Aboriginal people in BC's early settlement days.

The more I heard the stories of intermarriage and mutual support, the more I saw that dialogue could help build better relations between these important Vancouver communities. This project also helped inform the video *Cedar and Bamboo*, which I co-directed with Diana Leung, featuring stories from four people who have mixed Chinese and Aboriginal ancestry. In our community meetings and film screenings, I so often heard people exclaim, "We have so many commonalities between us!" And it was so often through sharing story—and food!—that we found our common ground. Projects like this go a long way by showing what we share and what we can learn from each other.

It was empowering to hear from Indigenous Elders and other community members who had so much knowledge and things to share, and such important perspectives. They taught us about the medicinal and food plants that have always grown here, that so many people see as weeds. Songs that have been on these lands for millennia. Stories of early prominent settlers, like Gassy Jack, having local Indigenous wives. There were so many "aha moments" when non-Native people heard these ignored stories for the first time. I saw planners' views of certain neighbourhoods and historic events shift when they heard Indigenous stories of these places and times. Soon one of my colleagues was pushing for a new statue of Gassy Jack's Squamish wife to be erected across the street from the famous statue! It was reassuring to see the impact these stories had on decision makers. Change the story, change the understanding.

THE DIALOGUES PROJECT

One day, while attending an Aboriginal community meeting in my capacity as social planner, an Elder shared his frustration that new immigrants coming to this land don't know about the First People.

"The problem starts when people come here," he said. "They aren't told that this is Indigenous land. We gotta change that."

I realized how right he was. When newcomers first get here, the information they're told is crucial to their understanding of their new home. But the information they get is so limited, because Indigenous people have been written out of the story. I wondered how different things might be if they had the chance to hear from Aboriginal people themselves. Soon after, I spoke with a colleague in Social Planning.

"Wouldn't it be great to have Aboriginal people and immigrants come together, so newcomers can hear from the people of the lands they are coming to?" I asked.

We dreamed about creating a means for dialogue between immigrants and Aboriginal people. A few years later, that same colleague raised the money to do just that, and in 2010, we launched the Dialogues Project. This groundbreaking project was guided by co-chairs from the Musqueam Nation, the Friendship Centre, and the Chinese community. It was a privilege to witness so much cultural sharing.

The project ran for almost two years. Mayor and Council were very involved and supportive, as were diverse community groups. Even former governor general of Canada Adrienne Clarkson and her husband, John Ralston Saul, became involved. During this time, the Musqueam First Nation hosted a citizenship ceremony. It was the first ever citizenship ceremony held on a BC reserve. It felt like the spirit of reconciliation was growing in Vancouver.

CITY OF RECONCILIATION?

Thanks to the tireless efforts of Aboriginal people and their allies, things were starting to change. In 2012, Vancouver finally had an Aboriginal committee, the Urban Aboriginal People's Advisory Committee, as a way for the urban (off reserve) Aboriginal population to liaise with local government. On Aboriginal Day 2013, the City of Vancouver became the first Canadian city to declare a Year of Reconciliation, with various initiatives and legacies planned. This was the year that the Truth and Reconciliation Commission of Canada came to Vancouver, where survivors of residential schools came to give their testimonies of what they endured. It was a time of healing and listening, as evidenced by the thousands who braved a downpour to be part of the Walk for Reconciliation. It was a massive event that showed just how far we have come from colonial misunderstandings that have kept people so disconnected. As many people later posted on social media: *All that rain was a cleansing. It's a new beginning now.*

During the Year of Reconciliation, Vancouver entered into

the first government-to-government meetings with the three local First Nations. This was a historic moment that I could only dream of when I started at the City and was continually told that local First Nations were "a federal issue." I had the privilege of facilitating the meeting with Tsleil-Waututh First Nation, and the respectful listening was incredibly uplifting. Vancouver now has an intergovernmental process with the three local First Nations.

In another historic move, in 2014 the City officially recognized "the modern city of Vancouver was founded on the traditional territories of the Musqueam, Squamish and Tsleil-Waututh First Nations and that these territories were never ceded through treaty, war or surrender." This recognition definitely helps do away with the empty land nonsense of the plaque on Hastings.

REMEMBER

I observe these various developments in Vancouver from a new town now. I have moved a forty-minute ferry ride away to raise my kids closer to the forest, in a smaller community. I continue to work for the City as a facilitator, as I am still committed to the work of decolonizing what will always be my city. While I am uplifted by the big shifts towards reconciliation that have happened, there is still a long way to go. There still aren't many visible recognitions of Vancouver being Coast Salish territory. Coast Salish people are still not adequately included in shaping what happens on their land. While the various reconciliation initiatives were happening, for example, a condo development was being planned at c̓əsnaʔəm, a Musqueam village and burial site. There had been no consultation with Musqueam. Despite their many efforts to stop this work from happening—asking the provincial government not to grant permits to dig on this nationally recognized heritage site—the digging commenced in 2012. Sure enough, intact Musqueam burials were found, and their ancestors' resting places were disturbed. As the digging went on, so did Musqueam's legal action to try to prevent further desecration. Families, leaders, Elders, allies, and community members marched, protested, and set up camp to keep vigil over the site.

Why was a permit granted to build condos on someone's village and burial grounds? Why did Musqueam have to set up roadblocks and protests, and then buy the land just to save their burial grounds? Musqueam had to literally write themselves onto the land—their name, their emblem—to remind people it's theirs. *Justice is promised. We are still watching.* This is their history; these are their ancestors. These are the struggles that remind us how much work there is to do. Had c̓əsnaʔəm been protected as an important part of Musqueam, rather than built on and intersected with roads and bridges, had the story and meaning of this place been fully visible and known, would there be more respect? I believe there would be. For that is the power of story.

· · ·

I hope all of us whose ancestors are elsewhere will learn the language of the land and connect to our new homes with a better understanding of the deep Indigenous roots everywhere we step. We are fortunate to make these places our home, and we can show our gratitude by always being mindful of the people who have so generously shared their land. We can be protectors ourselves, listening well, and respectfully finding our place in the many-storied land.

THE PERFECT TOOL

ZACHARIAS KUNUK

O NE SUNDAY NIGHT I was watching CBC—David Suzuki was on, talking about climate change in the Arctic. It was about scientists using wires to hook radio transmitters to the backs of snowy owls. The program was all about scientists, ice, permafrost. Nothing about us, the Inuit; nothing about the people who live up here or what we have to say. Still the same. And Suzuki's our buddy. It's still shocking to see these kinds of programs about the North, especially by our friends.

After seeing this show, I started talking with Ian Mauro, an environmentalist, and also a good friend of David Suzuki. I told him, "Man, David forgot us!" And he said that maybe it was an old program.

I hope so. Things should be changing.

But when you look at the weatherman doing weather reports on TV, they still report only St. John's to Vancouver. We're not important. We're a part of Canada but we're not important. When I'm down south, I still get asked, "Do you live in igloos? When you cry, do icicles come out of your eyes?" I say no, because we were taught to never cry outside.

The Franklin Expedition—that's another one where the southerners didn't listen to us. Elders talked about it. One Elder from here, Igloolik, talked about the time when Franklin's men at some point had the ship anchored to the land; the ice was pushing it and they were unloading a lot of stuff—wood, anything they could take out of this ship. The Elder's been to that place where there were millions of cans by the seashore; they were packed in the strong ice and it moved.

The Elders used to talk about that: where the current goes, that's where the ship goes. Even people in the area, I've heard stories from, because in the olden days their sense of smell was even greater than it is today—they could smell animals at a long distance. I heard a story from the Pelly Bay area where the Inuit were hunting. There were three men around the seal breathing holes just waiting. They could smell this odour in the air, and they saw these men walking, and they thought they were some kind of evil spirits and ran away to their own camp. They had their shaman investigate and he found out the men were hungry (in those days you communicated by sign language). So they started going to them and along the way they killed a polar bear. When they got to these men, the men just went after the bear meat.

That's oral history; there's nothing written about that. When I was growing up, still living on the land, my mother used to try to scare us about these white men. "When they're hungry," she'd say, "they're more fierce than us." That's probably from the experience of the Franklin days. Our parents used to try to scare us a lot. They'd say, "They're going to capture you and take you away!" Nowadays that's totally changed. My five-year-old granddaughter speaks perfect English—learned it from TV. A few years ago, when my granddaughter was just learning to speak, she was speaking Spanish from that *Dora the Explorer* show. Times are changing.

• • •

In our culture we observe and we learn; that was our teaching. We learned by watching our father tying up a sled, how he hitched the lines to the dog, how he untangled the lines. These things we just do and we learn. When the camera came it was the perfect tool to teach; we could just observe and roll the camera.

Hunting is still the same even though we use Skidoos as well as dog teams. We still hunt the same way because animals never change. They still have to eat; they follow their food chain and we follow them. In this area we have walrus year-round because we're in the flat lands and the water is shallow so there are a lot of mussels. Walruses are big animals, and if we constantly hunt them and get them, we are fine. They provide fat to heat our homes and a lot of meat; the meat we can't eat we feed to the dogs. We save it up to try to pass through the coldest part of the winter, when you can't hunt or go out too much—so we have a lot of meat cached up.

In our culture there were two systems: caribou hunters in the summertime, mainly for hides, and sea hunters trying to get oil and meat into the ground caches. Hunters travelled by the stars, by the current, by the snowdrifts, because the dominant wind used to be the North, and it cuts a trail. They didn't take geometry but they were cutting angles in the snowdrifts to get to where they were going. These were the scientific facts of the system. We also have different kinds of mittens and boots for when you're on the ice or on the land. Take the sealskin boot: men have to wear them out there on the salty sea, and they have to be waterproof—otherwise you're going to freeze your feet. We were very civilized and yet the Europeans didn't see us as civilized.

I went on a walrus hunt back in the 1980s—my first that I wanted to film. The hunters go way out to the sea and they come back with walrus. I wanted to go down, film the walrus, film how they hunt and butcher these two-tonne animals, how they pre-pare them and take them home. I hired a boat and two hunters and gassed the boat up, and had my camera on my shoulder. It's exciting; it's fun—you're down there with the walrus for the hunt, the butchering.

Then it was time to go home and there was no land in sight. "How are we are going to get home?" I asked. There was no land-ing site that I could see. But these guys, they knew—they looked at the sun and for the current, as it leaves a trail in the seaweed, with the leaves floating down in the water. They knew just by observing these things. We had to detour on the ice and we still got home. It's amazing knowledge, but thank god for GPS—our prayers were answered there!

In my school days I saw *Nanook of the North*—shot in northern Québec—and Inuit films made by anthropologists Asen Balikci and Peter Raymond. I grew up with this in my school days. I thought film was god-sent—even the early movies I saw at the community hall. I didn't know there was a camera and so many people behind the camera back then. I just thought it was real.

Now I know filming is all about faking it and faking the shots, and making it real at the editing table. But we try to do it as real as possible. We're very lucky in our company: we have costume makers that fit and clothe our actors, but down the road we won't be able to do that. In our production we have four Elders preparing the skins, cutting up the skins, teaching four young women—their apprentices—the whole time. Every time we're in production we do a little bit of teaching. We try a lot of things, because some of them we've just read about but have never seen. Like a coat made out of eider ducks—something we'd never seen but wanted. So we had eider ducks brought in; the women just sewed it up into the coat and we used that in *Atanarjuat (The Fast Runner)*. We wanted to learn how to make a caribou parka for winter, so we'd get the women to make patterns using their hands and strings; they do that even today to measure you up so you have a perfect outfit.

We are bringing things back from our culture. In my line of work we try to do it right. Real kamiks. Real boots. We make sure to use them. We try to respect the region, this kind of way of making clothes, because in another region they have a different style of clothing. Because you can tell the style just by looking at them.

With *Atanarjuat (The Fast Runner)*, when we were trying to make that, we ran into the law, because the Canadian financing system at that time was ridiculous. At that time it was Telefilm Canada and there was only $100 million for all filmmakers in the country. And only $2 million of that went to the Inuit and the immigrants. With $2 million you could make a movie, but each project in our category was capped at $100,000, so in a million years no one in our category would be able to make a movie. Lucky for us we had English people working with us doing English subtitles; that was the only thing that got us a piece of the pie. And the thing about the pie is, if I get a slice, other people don't, so that was quite an experience. But I never really got into that film financing system because my company, we are split in two—I'm on the creative side, and then there's the money side, and we don't try to mix them together. I want to do creativity; I want to learn more about my culture. How do shamans sing when they call their spirits? What songs do they sing to make a man beat a drum? Why do the stars and land have Inuktitut names while we Inuit all have biblical names?

I never thought about *Atanarjuat* being popular; it was our first try, after all—we did it in our own style, and we didn't follow the system. It took us six months to film, with a month or two off in between because we were trying to get all four seasons. It was our pilot project to see if we could do it. I never thought it would be that popular.

With the last film, I was looking for a story that I wanted to do—a conflict between the Inuit and Indians around the treeline. I had heard about Bloody Falls in the central Arctic, about the Franklin Expedition, and the Coppermine Eskimos who killed two ignorant priests who never learned their language, and the four-year hunt by the Royal Canadian Mounted Police. I saw pictures of them when they were on trial in Edmonton. But I wanted to do an old-time Indian war story with the Inuit, and I found one from the eighteenth century, from 1770. I was in northern Québec, in Nunavik, where Cree and Inuit live together. It's the most southern community of Inuit. The Cree call it Whapmagoostui and the Inuit call it Kuujjuaraapik. They are living under their two different land claims agreements, so the Inuit got housing and paved roads and port sites while the Cree got different housing systems and they didn't get paved roads. The community is still divided.

I was working with Neil Diamond, the Cree director, and we were looking for stories about how the Inuit and Indians used to fight. Neil was working with the Cree Elders and I was working with the Inuit Elders. It was July. While we were doing it they wanted to do a peace ceremony to commemorate 200 years of peace between the Cree and Inuit, and we were right in there. They wanted to do it in this certain area, and it took us four days to boat up there. But the Cree, under their land claim agreement, got Ottawa to fly them! The Inuit didn't get that, though, so we travelled by sea. The ceremony was at this beautiful waterfall, Nastapoka River—that's the Cree name for it. We were camping and I thought it was strange, because in July we have no night up here, but down there the night comes. After we got the stories and attended the ceremony, we filmed a little re-enactment drama there and we finished the film. It's called *Inuit Cree Reconciliation*.

For thirty years we've been at it on grants. It's tough but we won't stop. Right now we're working on a fictional drama movie. It's almost like *Atanarjuat*. It's based on true stories but it's fiction. We'll make it as real as we can, and we'll learn more about our ways—and tell our stories—in the process. Using the camera, the perfect tool.

TO KILL AN INDIAN

STEVEN COOPER *with* TWYLA CAMPBELL

Y DAD TOOK a lot of pictures when we lived in Coral Harbour, Nunavut, in the 1970s. One of the central figures in our lives there on Southampton Island was the Catholic priest. We were Jews in a half-Catholic, half-Protestant, traditional Inuit community with a population of 350 residents. Inuit dominated then, as they do now, with the total number of *qaloonaq* (non-Inuit) numbering a mere twenty. We, in particular, stood out and seemed to attract a lot of interest from the priest. I think he thought our redemption a personal challenge, one he was bound to fail, but he didn't know that. He cut a deal with us: my father would attend Catholic Mass at Easter and Christmas, and the priest would attend our home for Passover and Hanukkah.

One of the pictures in our extensive collection is of my then-four-year-old sister, sitting on the post office counter, dressed in a bright red parka with a fur-lined hood. The priest's arm circled her small body. I always thought it was a simple, yet beautiful picture. It always made me smile. We loved our time in Coral Harbour—or least the other four members of the family did. That sister was too young to have any memories of the place or time.

Knowing what I know now about the residential school system and the propensity for priests and laypeople to be perpetrators of so much sexual abuse, I now view that picture with some suspicion and discomfort. It didn't help that one of my clients, in his narrative on sexual abuse in the residential school system, made a passing reference to this particular priest. There was no residential school in Coral Harbour, so whatever abuse occurred at the hands of this particular priest, if any, would not have occurred within the context of this client's testimony. I didn't pursue this revelation because it had nothing to do with the client's claim, but I couldn't help but wonder what was going on in that priest's mind. Did he touch my sister? I'll never know, nor will she, because frankly she was too young to have any active memory from that time.

A government representative almost 100 years ago explained the purpose of the residential school system. It isn't the explanation that you often hear from government or from the churches today: that they intended to educate and acculturate First Nations children, to bring them into the modern era or allow them economic opportunities otherwise only available to people of European heritage. That bureaucrat may have been American, but his thoughts were echoed in the purpose and policy of the residential school system across Canada: to kill the Indian in the child. They could say things like that back then. They didn't need to couch reality in politically correct terms.

Most of the residential school attendees had their internal "Indian" or "Inuk" killed. The problem is that, much like the policy statement uttered a hundred years ago, the policy ended there. No one asked what would replace the parts killed, or who these children were to become as adults. Maybe the answer was so obvious no one asked the question. Nothing replaced that which was dead. Many of these children grew up not as Indians, First Nations, Métis, or Inuit. They grew up as hollow shells that turned to alcoholism, drug abuse, and criminal activity. They repeated the abuses they endured, and in turn abused others including, most devastatingly, their own families. The government residential school system created a social and intellectual desert in which nothing could grow. The children became adults who had children who similarly had nothing to nourish their spirit, their social awareness, or their confidence. They, like their parents and grandparents, were gutted and entered society repeating the cycle, over and over, whether or not they were students of that system.

The massive dike between the abused and the abusers only started to crack when a few very brave souls, truly the outliers, began to speak up—first in a whisper and then a shout for all to hear. It took one of them to contact me after a school reunion to bring me into the circle of knowledge.

This was my "aha moment" or perhaps its seed. In 1997, when my friend called to tell me of his residential school experience, I still knew nothing of this system. By 1974 we had already moved south to Manitoba in preparation for my bar mitzvah, and, coincidentally, because the only educational alternative for me in the Arctic was to go to a residential school. Unbeknownst to any of us, we left our friends to their fate. Eventually, I moved back to the North, to Hay River, where I finished high school and where I returned after law school to begin my practice.

This practice in the Northwest Territories included extensive court time with First Nations residential school graduates. The files I received centred on crimes related to addictions and violence and were committed by people who exhibited unexplained rage and a complete disconnect from societal norms. There was, sadly, a never-ending cycle of sexual crimes, often inflicted upon family members.

I wondered what the hell was wrong with these people. No one, not one person brought before the judge, ever mentioned a residential school or the horrors perpetrated there. The sort of anecdotes that every criminal defense lawyer wants to hear from their client were there, unspoken, but nothing was ever offered up to explain the accused's deviant behaviour.

People would ask me why the accused didn't disclose what had happened to them while they were alone with their lawyer or in the presence of a judge. It would seem an opportune time to explain or justify their actions. I have asked myself this very question for years. I was their friend, their classmate, co-worker, and for many, their defense lawyer in criminal court. Why didn't I know about this? Why didn't they tell me when I was trying to find the right words to say about them upon sentencing? Why didn't they use this as a bona fide explanation for their incorrigible behaviour? The answer didn't come to me overnight or all at once. Instead, it slowly dawned on me around 1997 when I represented the first group of survivors of the residential school system.

I came to the issue knowing nothing about the system and, as it turned out, very little about its survivors. As I learned about the system, the abuses, and the hierarchy that maintained both, the answer slowly formed in my mind. The system did two things very well: it not only killed the Indian in the child, it also undermined self-worth and confidence. It created a context where the people suffering felt they had no place to go to talk of their experiences and to seek healing. The indoctrination of these children by a church and government was swift and thorough. The primary aim was to make them docile. The secondary aim was to have them submit and comply. It was made abundantly clear they were to never question the authority of church or state. The children were deprived of the tools needed to understand their fate and to control their own destiny. The use of religion and European dominance made it virtually impossible for these children, even as adults, to confront the system that had gutted them.

This, then, is how we reflect on the place of the original churches in the communities in the Arctic. When the Catholic Church and various Protestant denominations first came north to seek new members for their flock, I have little doubt of their good intentions. I may not have, then or now, agreed with their goals, but I believe them to be entirely pure, however misguided.

The law of unintended consequences, however, resulted in the abusers cloaking themselves in authority. It was the perfect storm, one of horrendous proportions, for the children who were at the mercy of those with absolute power and unbridled perversions: *don't question us, don't tell on us, no one will believe you and you will spend eternity in damnation.* A few children told their parents who, more often than not, punished the children for what they, the parents, perceived as ridiculous and unfathomable accusations. Children couldn't phone their parents, and what few letters they sent were often edited or simply destroyed before receipt. Even if the letters got through, the parents often could not understand the language in which the letter was written. A small number of parents quietly hid their children from the authorities to avoid having them return to the houses of horror. In one incident, a parent shot a teacher's dogs in retaliation. Most students, though, had no recourse, no defenders, and no sanctuary. Year after year, the abuse continued until it just felt normal.

The residential school system combined two factors that led to the degree of abuse we now know occurred. First, it isolated the children from their parents in such an effective manner that sometimes the children had no communication with any member of their family for years at a time. Second, it indoctrinated the children and their families as to the incorruptibility and infallibility of the people and institutions that had taken the children in the first place—easier, to be sure, in the Catholic context, but effective at every level of church and state. These two factors, in my view and experience, contributed to a system that necessitated paying almost 100,000 living survivors some form of compensation.

True, "only" roughly 20 percent of that number (or 20,000) received compensation for specified acts of abuse, mostly sexual. Still, the rate of sexual abuse must be unprecedented in any First World country to date.

All of these factors had lifelong implications for a group of people who, until they were colonized, led happy, productive, loving lives. Yes, there were harsh times, but that was, and remains, true of every part of the world and for most of history. If you don't believe this to be the case, you need only go into a healed community to see how and what they have recovered.

In my outsider's view, some communities have been more successful than others in recovering the essence of being Inuit, First Nations, or Métis. One of my favourite communities is Repulse Bay, located directly on the Arctic Circle north of Winnipeg. Like any modern community, Repulse Bay has its problems, but unlike many Inuit communities, it has reclaimed its soul. This community has a different feel from some of the other less-successful communities I've visited. Repulse Bay's sense of culture is still alive despite the colonizers' attempts to destroy it. What is evident is the camaraderie, the sense of humour, the true understanding of what is important and what is not. The challenges of living in a hostile environment have given the Inuit a strong sense of perspective. They understand the importance of food, shelter, and family above all else. We colonists could learn much from them.

Among many other things, the fundamental misunderstanding of colonizers was that they felt they were filling a gap and raising Indigenous people from "savagery." They gave no notice to what they saw as the undeveloped culture, language, and society in the North. To their Eurocentric eyes, there was no society or culture worth preserving. They needed a clean slate; they needed to kill the Indian in the child. Because they didn't value or respect what was there, they saw a void to fill with their own concepts of right and wrong and what was important. Colonists have pursued this same modus operandi the world over, but rarely with such success.

Had they had even a modicum of understanding and foresight, they would have recognized they were destroying something wonderful. This destruction resulted in decades of intergenerational strife and discord. The colonizers managed to kill the Indian in the child while offering nothing to replace it. Without the guidance of parents and the grounding of tradition, without any societal norms, rules, or restrictions, those who survived the residential school system operated in a void. Ultimately, for many of them, this was filled with alcohol, drug abuse, and homelessness. These outcomes then led to the stereotypes so many non-Aboriginal Canadians grew up with, leading to even more racism. Even those of us who lived in the northern communities, who grew up with survivors of this abuse, had no idea of what had happened and the impact it had on our friends and neighbours. It was simply who they were. We never knew, nor could we even fathom, the real story. We had no way of knowing this was the fallout from the system designed by our government and carried out by so many churches. School textbooks were devoid of information and no one involved said a thing about it. It was a historical chimera.

Even today, most people don't know what happened to the First Nations and Inuit of this country despite the information that is now becoming available. I understand because I now know the story. I have spent almost twenty years hearing and documenting the abuses and guiding survivors through the compensation and healing process. I get it. I really do, but few Canadians have access to the people and history that allow this level of awareness.

I have seen what these people are made of, and of what they are capable; these people are survivors. I see beyond the person who sits on the street corner outside of the market selling the community newspaper, asking for money. The history of the residential school system is only now being taught—filtered, simplistic, and incomplete to be sure, but maybe, as our First Nations and Inuit move farther from the tragedy and our society comes to terms with the history, we will no longer act like nothing happened.

I'm not worried about our First Nations, Métis, and Inuit. I know that over time they will continue to take back what was taken from them. They will rebuild what was lost. It may not be in the same form, but it will be of the same nature. What I *am* worried about is the reaction of the non-Aboriginal people, the descendants of the colonizers who continue to see our Indigenous peoples' culture, language, and history as having little meaning or value. We as non-Aboriginals must recognize the historical injustices brought about by a system designed by our ancestors to achieve their goals, and that we all benefit from today. It served colonial purposes, but the price was paid by those people indigenous to this land we now call Canada. They, not we, have paid the price. The trivial compensation and half-hearted apologies offered by our government do little to offset their investment. We owe these people respect and understanding, and the opportunity to join our community on their own terms, not ours, and not those of our ancestors.

. . .

No nation can understand itself without a firm grasp of where it came from. Our nation has yet to fully teach its history and therefore cannot be said to understand itself. Until there is a substantial, sincere, and effective attempt to teach this history, the country will not—*cannot*—be whole. While we learn about Confederation, the battle of the Plains of Abraham, and the War of 1812, we do little more than take a passing glance at the less heroic times of our history, if my kids' textbooks are any guide. I wish my kids learned the real history of the residential school system in class and not just from their father who was privy to the information through his work. This historically cataclysmic event must take its proper place in our textbooks and classrooms. We need the next generation to know about, not just stumble upon, this formative event in our history.

As a post-colonial people governed by an as-yet colonial government, we need to understand what our nation almost lost in its quest for a homogeneous society. Our Indigenous people still chafe under the Indian Act and a bureaucracy that still threatens our First Nations, Métis, and Inuit as wards of the state. Change in our society, as always, must bubble up from the people.

. . .

Our society depends on historical integrity. In this country we have a record of apologies and reconciliation, but what we also need is acceptance and action. When all Canadians understand the impact of what the residential school system did to our Indigenous peoples, only then will the prime minister's 2008 apology for the operation of this horrid system really mean something—because what is an apology worth if you don't understand what you're apologizing for? Reconciliation will flow naturally when this happens.

They say it's never too late to learn, and in that I remain hopeful. When every Canadian knows about the Indians who were killed in the children, when every Canadian, no matter their heritage, accepts what colonization did to our First Nations, only then will our country be whole—an entire nation healed. *That* will be Canada's a-ha moment.

TWO-STEP

KATHERIN EDWARDS

"I DON'T THINK WE can go this way," Devon calls to us. She's crawled around a large rock to take what we all agreed looked like a direct route to the cave. Gail's behind her, then it's me.

"Seriously?" I say. "Seriously?" Clutching at dirt and puffing from the near-vertical climb, we sidle up to a pathless rocky crevice. The chalk-white mountain looms above, and the eyelash slit in the middle seems so far away. A single bird floats above us as failure flutters through my mind. *We've simply taken a wrong turn,*

I tell myself. *We'll regroup. We'll retrace our steps and figure out where we went wrong. We'll try again.*

Back in our hometown of Kamloops, in the interior of British Columbia, two women from Tk'emlups te Secwepemc (the Kamloops band of the Shuswap Nation), along with their family and friends, are walking their own tough trail, eager to turn a twenty-year-old dream into reality. Carol Camille and her mother-in-law, Evelyn, have searched for years for a place to serve up a first-of-its-kind Aboriginal food restaurant in the city. In a low-slung white building just east of the centre of town, less than a block away from where I live, is their adventure, a restaurant they'll call the Painted Pony Cafe. Behind papered-up windows, it is on a solid path toward its opening date.

Our trek begins with a guidebook entry for a day trip to Savona Mountain. Approximately forty-five minutes west of Kamloops and home to "authentic cave paintings," the book describes the mountain as an eroded shield volcano, and the trail (the trail!) leading to the caves follows eroded volcanic ridges. We think it's going to be easy, and for the first twenty minutes it is. Wide pine path. Stroll through the woods. Chirping birds, the odd squirrel. But up close, when you lace up your boots and step into the deep landscape, southern BC is definitely rougher.

Where the trail first takes a more vertical slant we stop for a snack. Lichen on twisted deadfall, red twig dogwood, and thick stalks of mallow stand tall like exclamation points at the end of a long sentence, as if the land is surprised we've ventured onto it.

Back on the trail, each step becomes more deliberate and slow as we balance on shale and rubble bound by a fine slick of dust. Soon it's a straight-up lung-collapsing hike. I taste blood at the back of my throat. The land is dry. We time-out. Regroup. Climb. Rest some more by leaning against the mountain. Clutching thin blades of grass, we pull ourselves along. And maybe because the sky is deliciously blue, and a sweet breeze twirls the tops of the pines, we keep going. The cave appears, disappears, until finally a narrow goat trail through a large split rock opens up. By the time we're near enough to see the caves less than nine metres ahead, we're on hands and knees, crawling, spreading our mass and staying low. Not unlike the stunted surrounding shrubs, we are searching for stability.

* * *

Carol Camille, co-owner of the newly opened Painted Pony Cafe, is an advocate of sharing, and food is at the centre of her belief. She's determined that sharing has the potential to take down barriers. The logo for the Painted Pony is a profile image of a horse's head and neck, painted in deep brown, blacks, and greys. The mane is composed of a row of feathers in various sizes arcing like a crescent moon, and it looks as if the horse is about to take flight in its feathered headdress. When I ask Carol about the name and logo, she tells me horses were prominent in her family. "Journeys are made with horses. We opened this place in the year of the horse." It's November 29, 2014, and Carol and Evelyn are ready to share traditional Aboriginal fare with anyone who walks through the front door. Cedar plank smoked salmon, elk stew, deer steak, and a dozen kinds of Evelyn's famous bannock grace the menu. The paper is off the windows and light streams into the new restaurant. Their dream is a reality.

. . .

We reach the cave, breathless, excited, but cautious too. We agree that the space doesn't feel entirely safe. Air and rock. This does not feel comfortable, and I'm in awe of those who walked on this land as if it were home. Afraid of tipping over and tumbling down the rubbly terrain, I concentrate on keeping my weight to the topside of the mountain. Tired but giddy, we congratulate each other on our accomplishment and break out the food. A quiet peace follows as we check out the view. From a height of 1200 metres the alfalfa fields carved from the forest below us snake like a green river through the valley. Deciduous trees at the pinnacle of autumn splendour shimmer golden-yellow, while a sway of power lines cuts through a swath of evergreens, reminding me of how tightly modern civilization is wired together. From nearby a bird chirps. Then, before we explore further, we line up for a selfie. We three have made it. We are here.

Savona Mountain rises like a huge, split, prehistoric thunderegg, and the crack we are about to explore yawns open to reveal its goods. The cave itself, more rubble than solid rock, holds a cache of smaller scattered geodes. The mouth is on a downward slant, and while you can almost stand upright, your feet remain clenched at a forty-five degree angle. The horizontal fissure horseshoes around a rocky point in the centre, and to reach the pictographs on the other side, you can go one of two ways: you can either crawl deep into the darkness behind the stand of rock (and possibly the home of bats, rats, or cougars) or attempt the narrow trail outside the cave. Boulders and shale cut along the edge of the mountain, and one slip off this narrow path means a fall into a deadly mix of rocks and trees. It's a strange game of "choose your fear." I bend in half and prepare to boomerang through the cave. It smells rank. I scamper out, knowing eventually I'll have to crawl back the way I came. Yes. Crawl back.

It takes a few moments to spot the paintings, but there, close to the edge of the opening, amongst all the pitted and clumped stones on the roof of the cave, is a flat boulder, and it is here First Nations people made their mark. Possibly members of the Secwepemc Nation created these paintings. Either way, the drawings are so vivid and brilliant in colour, even from a distance they look as if they were recently executed. It's likely the ochre, mixed with salmon eggs or animal fat, has attributed to this brightness. Composed of iron oxide found in the earth, red ochre is also derived from hematite—the name coming from the Greek root word *hema*, meaning blood. Blood from the land. Proof there was someone here before. Long before settlers rode through this land, long before machines churned the earth, someone climbed to these rocks and painted their day. I imagine fingers dipping into a container, staining red, recording on rock.

* * *

It's February 2015 when I finally step inside the Painted Pony for breakfast. It's a dull morning and slush lines the streets from days of melting snow. A jaunty tune plays quietly, and from the kitchen a woman hums along. The smell of bacon and bannock flows through the warm restaurant. I seat myself near the large curving window, and a young server, busy counting a float at the next table, says, "Be with you in a minute." The view opens to an outdoor patio with a large pile of dirty snow. Coffee arrives in an oversized ceramic mug along with sealed creamers in a silver mini-bucket. I glance at the menu. There's the Camp Special (deer steak with eggs), the Coastal Pony (salmon cakes and poached eggs), but it's the item at the top of the menu that catches my eye. I know it's probably a colossal amount of food, so when I hand back the menu I say, "Don't judge me, but I'll take the Painted Pony Special."

The server giggles. "Are you kidding? It's my favourite."

As I wait for my order I note the pony motifs. They are every-where. Ponies painted on the floor dance below a large original painting of a blue pony on the wall. The western-style hanging light has numerous shades with silhouettes of horses. I'm still counting horses when breakfast arrives. There's a bright twist of orange like a slice of sun on a plate of three cheese-topped eggs. Bacon, bologna, hash browns, and bannock circle the dish, and it's delicious.

Carol Camille is one busy lady, and we agree to meet a few days later to sit and talk. She has a long black braid and stunning green eyes that match her T-shirt with a caption that says MY GRANDMOTHER MAKES BETTER BANNOCK THAN YOUR GRANDMOTHER. Trained as a psychologist, Carol works seven days a week, fourteen-plus hours at a number of different jobs. She's clear-eyed, calm, and, above all, present. When I ask why here, why now, she looks out at the main street of Kamloops and says, "It's where we're supposed to be."

* * *

The cave paintings are difficult to see, so near to the edge and on the ceiling of the cave that it's not until later when I take a close look at my photos that I can see the pictographs clearly. There are three stick figures grouped across one panel. Two of the figures have what look like spears in their hands while the third does not. Scattered between them are four animals with horns. Three of the four are outlines only, while the fourth is solidly coloured. Are these figures mountain goats, sheep, or deer? Is the red-filled animal their next meal? The figure closest to this animal is the only one not holding a spear. Whatever the purpose, the message in the pictographs is clear: *We. Were. Here.*

It occurs to me these pictographs ought to be shielded somehow, and it seems the government agrees—perhaps a little too much. Colonialism reared its head in the form of a management plan when the Savona Caves became part of the Mount Savona Provincial Park in October of 1999. The management direction statement for the Thompson Nicola Region District designated these parks as protected areas in May 1996, and identified the caves as a protected zone under the heading of cultural heritage. Released a mere fifteen years ago, this need to continue to lay claim to First Nations Sites and indicate it's ours feels wrong. How is it possible this authentic vestige of permanent culture belongs to us? Yet there is hope—not in our hand opening to "them" on the basis of government documents, but perhaps theirs opening to "us." It's possible that we need to see what we have in common to coexist and live in a land that is not meant to be owned so much as shared. And "share" is the key word.

And that's where Carol Camille fits into this picture. We meet on a Sunday afternoon between jobs. The snow has melted and the sun is shining. Settling in at the same table where I'd had breakfast, I explain the purpose of this essay while Carol quietly explains the why of the restaurant. "We share everything and we give our best. There's no question. It's just what you do." And when Carol and her family offer up their talents and share their recipes, it's clear it's done with love, affection, and good will. "Can't cook if you're angry," she tells me, "it comes out in the food."

I'm curious about the patrons, and when I ask the percentage of Caucasian to First Nations she says, "About fifty-fifty." She pauses, and then adds, "But I can always tell when an order comes back. If it's First Nations then they take what they are given knowing we give our best. A Caucasian tends to say, 'I want it done this way, with that . . .'"

Silence hangs.

"Then we're still demanding," I say. It's not a question but a statement. We have claimed the land and her resources. Foisted our culture on others. Bulldozed with our ideas to create our ideal and even here, even in this restaurant owned by First Nations, the insistence on having it our way hasn't stopped. As Carol and her mother-in-law have held out their hands in an offer of sharing, I feel grateful but inadequate to give back. If only I had something equally valuable to offer. The concept of sharing seems to be something that doesn't come naturally to many of us.

A few weeks later we decide to try out the dinner fare. I feel the very least I can do is support Carol and Evelyn's dream, not to mention that there are items on the menu that can only be had at the Painted Pony. When I call up to ask if they take reservations, I falter on the phone.

Reservations. Loaded word.

The person on the other end simply says yes, they take them.

We return and again, as we walk into the restaurant, I'm drawn to the horse motifs. This time it's the stick-on outlines above the windows. The three different styles, all depicting figures on horses, look a little like pictographs or a line of brands.

As we pass by the table where Carol and I sat, I'm reminded of how our conversation ended. There was a moment of awkward silence when we reached the point of "What now?" At that moment, the world I inhabited felt futile. Carol rose and returned with a box of tissues. She placed it on the table between us. A few minutes later her granddaughter brought us tall glasses of ice water. Carol and I looked at each other, and then out at the dirty sidewalk. I blinked hard, but neither of us could stop the tears. One idea stood firm: *We were still demanding.*

Finally the words came, small and useless. "I don't know how to help with the healing. I don't know what to do."

Carol nodded towards my notebook. "You're doing it," she said. "You're writing about it."

I made a few notes and I closed my book. None of it felt enough.

"You know you're doing it too," I said. "You're offering up your recipes and culture. And you're sharing . . ."

Close to ninety minutes had gone by, quick as if time stopped, and Carol had another job to get to. When we stood, I moved towards her for a hug. "Thank you for your emotions," Carol said. We folded into each other, keenly aware of the richness of that moment.

*   *   *

The next time I'm there, I decide I'm going to try the Indian Ice Cream. Though to call it ice cream is a stretch. The dessert known as Hooshum is made from the orange and red fruit of the soapberry bush found here in the interior of BC. The treat is whipped up into a mousse-like froth and sweetened with sugar, and it arrives in a tall glass on a side plate. On first taste it's bitter, foreign on the tongue, much like its Secwepemc name *Sxesem*. I have never tasted anything like it. It tastes as if the land has been processed in a blender. Pink in colour, the more you have the more curiously addicting it is—and oddly comforting knowing this treat is made from a deciduous shrub that was unharmed and left in its original location.

The Latinate botanical name for the soapberry plant is *Shepherdia canadensis* and as difficult to pronounce as its Secwepemc name. Yet perhaps its description in a guide of common plants is what's most startling. *An unarmed spreading shrub.* It says much about settlers, armed with tools and animals, quick to brand and claim ownership over a land we knew little about. Listening to those who came before wasn't part of any deal. So today, to walk into this good land and puff our way to witness the first brand in a cave feels unsettling. To *be* of this good land feels foreign. We have not settled properly because we have not looked at what the First Nations people experienced, offered, or what they're offering now. We changed the design of the earth and cultivated it to grow food, not once stopping to recognize native species of plants. We demanded what we knew, then demanded for more of what we didn't.

There are plenty of definitions for the word "settle"; however, the one I prefer is "to come to rest, as from flight." As a bird settles. To soar above the land, take stock, perch without harming, settle without ownership, and be grateful without exploitation.

On the corner of 7th and Victoria Street two women have settled. It is, after all, as Carol says, "where we belong."

It makes me wonder how and where I belong.

ECHO

CAROL SHABEN

T HE MOST EXOTIC person in my small town high school was an Aboriginal girl named Echo. There were fewer than 300 students in my school and a mere 3,000 in my town, but if there'd been ten times that many, Echo still would have stood out. Not only was she statuesque—at five feet ten inches tall she overshadowed the other girls in the school—she was beautiful. Her black hair fell in a luxurious curtain past her shoulders and a hem of bangs feathered thick eyebrows above dark almond-shaped eyes. Beneath them were high cheekbones, strong and striking, yet softened by a delicate ridge of nose and full lips pursed in a shy half-smile. When she did smile, her teeth were perfect and white against amber-brown skin, and her entire face seemed to radiate a quiet knowing.

There was something mysterious and reserved about Echo. Unlike the Caucasian girls in my town, whose rough and tumble younger brothers I endured during games of kick the can in The Circle—the solitary cul-de-sac in our town—or whose moms I often spied, heads half swallowed beneath the alien-looking domes of hairdryers at Leonarda's Beauty Salon, I never met Echo's siblings or family. Not once did I visit her home for a birthday party or sleepover. In fact, I didn't know for sure where her house was despite the fact I lived in a town where you could cycle the streets in less time than it took to have a passing sidewalk conversation, and where everyone seemed to know your business before you did.

I had a vague idea that Echo lived somewhere east of town, down a stretch of tar-striped prairie highway on the other side of the town campsite. How could it be that I'd never once thought to ask? Our friendship found its footing in high school and seemed to be completely contained by it. On occasion we hung out together over lunch hours on the hard tiled bench inside the school's front entrance watching a parade of students stomping in from the wintry cold, the stained snow of their shoes melting into sodden dark doormats. In English we sat next to each other, diligent, hard-working students sometimes catching each other's eye to smile at the sophomoric antics of the boys in class. If paired up in science, we'd dip our heads together to dissect a lab specimen, filled with awe at its tiny, perfect innards. On rare occasions, our conversation would rise above the standard fare of high school foibles and infidelities, and slide towards our future dreams: mine to be a lawyer and defend the downtrodden, hers to find happiness and peace of mind. I held our friendship like a quiet secret. As a member of one of two Arab families in the town, I felt an affinity with Echo, an uncommon off-white identity. I considered myself an outsider too. After all, my family didn't worship at a church and we weren't allowed to eat the pork hot dogs at hockey games or order the bacon cheeseburger that was all the rage at the Denny's Drive-In.

But it wasn't just our shared "otherness" that attracted me to Echo. There was something regal and reserved about her that drew me out of the dusty shell of isolation I often felt on the northern Canadian prairie. It was as if she and I were somehow apart from the white Anglo mainstream.

The looking glass I'd fashioned for myself in high school brought this image into sharper focus at university. I recall studying a unit on the First Nations in a course called "Contemporary Issues in Political Philosophy." During one discussion I felt personally affronted when a classmate, a young woman who'd grown up in the city, attributed the current problems faced by "Indians" to laziness and alcoholism. I was so incensed that I begged the professor to let me bring in a knowledgeable guest speaker to address the class. One of the most memorable moments of my entire undergraduate education was watching this speaker, a soft-spoken, insightful man of forty and government colleague of my father, systematically dispel the many stereotypes held by students who, I surmised, had not had the benefit of growing up with a friend like Echo. In particular, I relished the moment of perfect poetic justice that culminated in the heated debate between the racist young woman and my guest:

Young woman: *I don't think—*

Guest speaker: *Exactly.*

I hung on to that triumph like a rare, bright penny. It became the signature coin in a change purse jingling with social justice causes. I was nineteen and determined to save the world—one disenfranchised population at a time. And when it came to the First Nations, I felt I had an insider's perspective.

I can't say how such a self-indulgent sensibility lodged itself so deeply into my subconscious, but it was years before I thought to question it. The impetus came just last summer when I received an email via my website. The sender, an Aboriginal woman I'll call Rose, had recently read my book and wanted my opinion on a story. It turns out that the story was hers.

Government authorities had taken Rose from her family and placed her in an orphanage when she was three years old. The day she arrived, the nuns had removed and disposed of her clothes, bathed her in kerosene, given her a crude haircut and uniform, and told her never again to speak her language. She'd met dozens of other brown-skinned girls identically shorn and clothed, but it wasn't until that night after she'd been placed in a crib—one of several lined up against the wall in a yawning roomful of beds— that a terrible reality started to dawn. When Rose laid her head down and looked through the bars, inches away was another girl her own age crying noiselessly, her tears sliding down her cheeks to dampen the mattress below. That's when Rose began to realize she would not be going home.

The childhood that followed was sadly similar to that of many of Rose's generation—a harsh, regimented institutional upbringing, physical and sexual abuse, and the loss of family, culture, and Aboriginal identity—with one extraordinary exception. Sometime during her five years at the orphanage Rose developed vitiligo, a skin disorder in which the body's pigment-producing cells are destroyed. In the decade after she left the orphanage at age eight, and endured five different foster homes until age eighteen, an ever-expanding territory of white colonized the brown landscape of her skin. As fate would have it, by the time Rose was nineteen she was, from the perspective of anyone who saw her, a white woman.

Rose's story captivated me. It was eerily reminiscent of the experience of John Howard Griffin, a white Texan who travelled through the American South "passing" as a Black man. Griffin—who transformed his appearance with the help of large doses of anti-vitiligo medication, and long lie-ins under an ultraviolet lamp—recounted his six weeks as a "Negro" in a 1961 memoir entitled *Black Like Me*. The book was not only an explosive exposé on American racism, it was a seminal and enduring work that has helped generations of white Americans understand the impact that their prejudices and repressive practices imposed on their African American brethren. If Griffin's brief ordeal inhabiting the skin of a Black man could have such an eye-opening impact, surely the story of Rose's unprecedented transformation from a shunned and abused Aboriginal youth to living the next five and a half decades as an openly accepted white woman would create a seismic shift in attitude.

Meeting Rose felt serendipitous, as if her choosing me to tell her story affirmed a connection that had begun decades before through my friendship with Echo. This feeling gained greater purchase when Rose confided in me that a New York literary agency had previously offered to buy her story and put her in touch with five potential writers. Rose had interviewed them all but felt none understood her situation in a way that gave her confidence to move forward.

Determined to uphold the faith Rose had placed in me, I immersed myself in research, not just interviewing her, but reading books and articles, combing First Nations websites, subscribing to news feeds, and even enrolling in an eight-week Indigenous Cultural Competency training program. The program began by teaching aspects of Canada's history I'd never learned in high school or university: chilling facts about Indian residential schools and Indian hospitals; restrictive government legislation such as the Indian Act (which formed the basis for South Africa's apartheid policies); and the crippling consequences and legacy of colonization. I added it all to the arsenal of knowledge with which I would write Rose's story. Next, the program turned its focus to self-awareness, asking students to reflect on white and Christian privilege. I held steadfastly to my worldview: I wasn't white; I was Arab. I wasn't Christian; I was raised a Muslim. I could relate to discrimination. To stereotyping. My affinity with our Indigenous population that had taken root in a tiny northern prairie town remained intact. I sailed on to the next assignment: writing about my family's history settling in Canada.

That's when something unexpected happened. I'd always been

proud of my status as a third-generation Canadian and, in particular, of the sacrifice and harsh living conditions my grandparents had endured so I could prosper. They left Lebanon after the First World War for the promise of free land and a better life in Canada. How could it be that I'd never until that moment—until tasked with one seemingly simple assignment—realized that the land upon which my Canadian forefathers had laid the foundation for my future was not "free" at all? Like the location of Echo's home, it was something I had never even considered.

That moment of realization should have been a wake-up call. Instead, I hit the snooze button and plowed forward on Rose's story. With her permission, I pitched a feature article on her life to a national magazine, telling her it was the best way to build interest in a book. We continued to meet and talk, but as the deadline approached my focus turned increasingly inwards toward the solitary task of writing.

"Can I read what you've written?" Rose asked.

"Not yet," I replied. I wanted to get a first draft under my belt. I'd already told Rose about the opening scene—something my editor had suggested would act as a perfect metaphor for her story—and she'd seemed hesitant. In that scene, Rose is fourteen and stands naked in the tiny outhouse behind a southern prairie farmhouse, her third foster home. Beneath her slim brown feet is a mat of newsprint she has draped across the rough wooden floorboards and toilet. On its closed seat rests a small tin of "neutral lightest beige" house paint.

Rose shivers—from excitement, not cold—as she dips a brush into the paint and bends to sweep a swath of it from the top of her left foot to her knee. The effect is even better than she'd hoped; the pinto-patterned patches of her skin now uniformly white. She finishes painting one leg then the other, moving on to her arms and torso. A gurgle of happiness erupts and, for the first time in her life, Rose looks forward to tomorrow. That's because with every stroke of the brush, she sees herself becoming white.

"Is it necessary to include that part?" Rose asked after I told her about the beginning of the article. I thought I understood her reticence. After all, she was now in her seventies and the scene might be embarrassing. Yet I never asked. I was intent on her seeing my point of view.

"It's really important that we don't sanitize things," I said, though I had no recollection that I'd used the word "sanitize."

Rose reminded me of it later when our relationship began to unravel. I shudder now to think of how offensive that word must have sounded to a woman who'd been bathed in kerosene on her first day in government care and whose culture society had labelled savage and dirty for hundreds of years. Somehow I'd been oblivious.

• • •

The day Rose and I had the conversation that put the chill on our relationship, we had been collaborating for more than six months. Her request that I cancel the article, just as I was sprinting to finish the draft, seemed to come out of nowhere. Looking back, had I been more sensitive, more attuned, I should have seen it coming as clearly as a thunderstorm across parched prairie.

At the time, however, Rose's concerns made no sense: that the article had too much detail; that it would undermine publishing opportunities for a book in the same way that an overly inclusive movie trailer sapped audience interest in the movie; and that she didn't want to shame the people who had abused her, or hurt their children.

I tried desperately to dissuade her, to reason my way back to the firm footing I'd once held. The harder I tried, the more I found the ground beneath me dropping away like dry earth eroding from a cliff's edge.

"Give her time," my agent advised.

So I did. I sent Rose an email saying the decision was hers to make and that I would respect it, but not before laying out the evidence that well-written articles *do* lead to book publishing deals. I offered to change people's names to protect their identities, promised to follow up with her on a specific date and, in what I considered an act of magnanimity, I attached a copy of my draft article hoping that in reading what I'd written, she would find her answer.

I was right. Rose did find her answer, but not the one I thought she would. Before the date I'd specified, she sent me an email. After further thought, she explained, she didn't think we'd be good collaborators.

"Our ideas are different," she wrote. "This was your book, written in your voice."

Her words now, to me, embody the essence of Canada's long and unequal relationship with our First Nations. Like having a childhood friend whose home I'd never stepped foot in, there was something in my connection with Rose that eluded me. It took weeks, however, for me to realize this, and it was longer before I began to understand that just because my skin was a shade darker and I'd grown up with an Aboriginal friend, I did *not* have an insider's perspective.

The more I thought about my long-held paradigm, the more its fabric became gossamer thin. I'd left my hometown more than thirty years earlier, yet in all that time I'd had no significant friendships with First Nations individuals. And what of Echo, the young woman on whose shoulders I'd long stood to claim my vaulted viewpoint? I'd seen her just once since high school and it was only by chance. We ran into each other on the University of Alberta campus, and though overcome with fond remembrance, we had only a brief conversation. I can't recall what we talked about, only that I'd been surprised to see glittering rows of piercings that lined the lobes of both ears. My lasting impression of that fleeting encounter was that each puncture marked an experience I had not endured and could never fathom.

I lost track of Echo after that, only finding her again seven years ago through social media. I gave her a brief synopsis of my rather mainstream life—married, one child, and career—and asked for her news. It was a few years, perhaps longer, before she wrote back. She apologized for the delay, saying she had her "crazy reasons" and that she'd "been on a bit of a rollercoaster in this life."

I wanted to ask Echo what she meant, but I never found the courage. Our correspondence remained light and sporadic, and I recently discovered that she had started her own business working with dogs. I couldn't help but wonder if her choice was because dogs were more loyal and constant than the people in whom she had placed her trust.

. . .

Early in my relationship with Rose, before I'd destroyed the trust she'd placed in me, I asked why her mother had allowed a complete stranger from the government to walk into her wilderness home and take her baby away.

"Native people, we acquiesce," Rose said.

On that score, however, I like to think she was wrong. Rose did not simply hand over her remarkable story to someone she felt would appropriate it. And thoughher story is not mine to tell, I am grateful to her for forcing me to acknowledge my long-held biases and beliefs. I am also humbled by Rose's capacity, in spite of all she has suffered, to see the good in encounters with others and never close a door. In the final line of her email she told me to take good care of myself, and said that if I wanted to meet for a cup of coffee, she would welcome it.

I'm not sure if I'll take Rose up on her offer, but a few days ago I exchanged telephone numbers with Echo. When we talk, I plan on asking a lot of questions I should have asked a long time ago, starting with where she lived when we were kids.

MOTHER TONGUES

KATHERINE PALMER GORDON

LET'S SAY YOUR first language is English. It could be French, if you prefer. This is Canada, after all. Either way, English or French, it's your first language, part of who you are.

You learned it as an infant; it's the fundamental way you express yourself as an adult. You understand every nuance of meaning in each word and phrase, everything written between the lines. When you hear it and speak it—something you get to do every day in this officially bilingual country—your connection to your nationhood and culture is nourished, and thrives.

That's easy to take for granted here. Press one for English, *tapez deux pour le français*—we all know what that means. It's part of the national identity, about as Canadian as it gets. That's what language does for us: it identifies us, anchors us to place and heritage and culture, and allows us to communicate effortlessly with our fellow speakers so they understand us with no need to divine further meaning or intent.

For the one and a half million Canadian Indigenous people whose mother tongues *aren't* officially recognized in this country, however—whose languages aren't taught in schools, or celebrated in spelling bees and crossword puzzles and board games and writing contests, or used in hospitals and dental offices and government services—it's a different matter. What number do you press to speak in Hulq'umin'um, or Cree, or Mi'kmaq?

The likelihood today of a First Nations person in Canada hearing their language spoken on a daily basis is small. The 2011 census reported that only 15 percent of Indigenous people in Canada still regularly use their original languages. In British Columbia, home to more than half the country's original languages, six have become permanently silent. The remaining thirty-two, spoken by just 5 percent of the First Nations population of the province, are at serious risk of joining them.

Does that matter in a country where the languages of government, commerce, education, entertainment, and society in general are English and French? Why pay any attention to dialects that are all but forgotten save by a small fraction of the population? Why on earth should we care?

Because it does matter, and it matters deeply. We must pay

attention, because as a country we cannot afford to lose any more original languages. If the peoples of Canada are ever to achieve understanding and reconciliation between each other, no matter which language we speak, then we *must* care about the full revival of these languages, and the right of all First Nations people in the country to learn and speak them fluently: the languages of the Mi'kmaq, the Miliseet, the Algonquin, Seneca, Cree, Mohawk, Anishinaabe, Dene, Innu, Ojibway, Métis, Ktunaxa, Haida, and Hulq'umin'um Nations, and all of the other peoples whose names illuminated the map of Canada long before the country existed, eons before the English and French came.

I care, because my understanding of how vital an influence language has on someone's life is intensely personal. When I immigrated to Canada from New Zealand in 1989, I immediately tripped over the fact that while English might be my first language, it was a completely different idiom from Canada's version. My rounded Kiwi vowels were constantly misunderstood. I couldn't order a glass of water in a restaurant without the server saying, "Pardon me?" several times. I'd get into trouble using slang that was innocent to me, but meant something rude in a Canadian setting. Sometimes I'd get angry, snapping at checkout servers who couldn't understand me. It was enormously tiring; some nights I would come home to my Toronto apartment and switch on BBC television, just for the relief of hearing English spoken in a more familiar way.

I eventually got used to the differences, of course, but I stayed on the back foot in conversation for years; the cultural references in this country were so alien to me that even twenty-five years later I still sometimes have to ask what people are talking about. Occasionally I will forget myself, and fall afoul of certain words and phrases. My blunt Kiwi sense of humour can still get me into trouble if I'm not careful.

Back then, I suppose I took it for granted that it's just the way it is when you speak a different language—or in my case, speak the same language differently. Then, a few years ago, it happened all over again—this time, in French, and with a far more visceral and profound impact on me and my sense of cultural identity, of who I am and my place in the world.

In 2007, I visited my mother's side of the family in France for the first time. Once again, I was culturally lost at sea in a world of words and slang and cultural references I couldn't understand. Because I hadn't learned my mother's original language, French, as a child, I'm not fluent in it. I found it difficult to communicate effectively. I stumbled in conversation, missed out on meaning, and didn't get the jokes. My pronunciation was poor and frequently misunderstood; I felt inadequate, inferior, and was constantly anxious.

I had become involved with First Nations language revitalization in British Columbia a few years previously, through a combination of working in treaty negotiations, sitting on the board of the First Peoples' Cultural Foundation, and writing about it. I understood the theory very well. But now the sheer importance of language as it underpins personal and cultural desires, needs and potential, on one's own terms—and ultimately, the ability just to get through the day—really hit home. For the first time, I was experiencing that intimately for myself.

I returned home from France saddened and longing to be fluent in my mother's language. I'm not saying that I suddenly wanted to speak French *instead* of English. I have English blood in my veins as well as French; speaking English is part of who I am and essential to my daily life. But it's also not a substitute for a strong connection to the French part of my heritage. What I really wanted, what I still crave, is to speak *both* languages with equal ease and pride, to finally feel complete in my sense of my heritage and cultural identity.

It's easy, from that position, to understand the desire on the part of First Nations people to reclaim their languages. Knowing the history behind their loss of the languages, and the impact that has had not only on First Nations themselves but on Canada as a country, it's also not hard to appreciate why reclaiming the languages matters, and why we should all care about that, regardless of our own experiences.

The reason those languages are no longer in widespread daily use in Canada lies in Canada's residential school system. Over the course of more than a century, 150,000 children across the country were forcibly taken from their homes and families and sent to government-funded, church-run residential schools, to be indoctrinated in settler teachings, beliefs, and ways of life. They were forced to speak English or French, and brutally punished for speaking their own languages. The goal was to interrupt the transmission of language from generation to generation, thereby eventually extinguishing them—and along with them, cultural world views that were in conflict with those of the settlers. The last school closed in 1996. By then, the damage had been well and truly done.

Those who escaped the residential system didn't have a much easier experience. They suffered systemic racism and were taught subjects completely foreign to their experience, often utterly incomprehensible to them. SELILIYE, from Tsartlip First Nation on the Saanich Peninsula of southern Vancouver Island, went to public school in the 1960s. She also wasn't allowed to speak her mother tongue, SENĆOŦEN. "It was a nightmare for me," she recalls. "We were taught Latin instead. I had no idea what any of it meant. I would get called a dumb Indian. I dreaded going." Eventually, she simply stopped. "There was no point," she says sadly. "I learned nothing at all."

All these children deprived of their languages over the years were—and in many cases still are—the victims of what is now a generally accepted truth: remove the language from the child, and the emotional, cultural, and academic costs are enormous in terms of disproportionately high school dropout rates, as well as unemployment, addictions, crime, and suicide rates.

In 2007, University of Victoria associate professor of psychology Christopher Lalonde co-published a report starkly titled "Aboriginal language knowledge and youth suicide." Lalonde and his colleagues studied 150 First Nations communities in British Columbia. They discovered that language had more predictive power in anticipating suicide rates than any other standard socio-economic indicator like poverty or unemployment. The results of the research were arresting: "Rates dropped to zero in communities in which at least half the members reported a conversational knowledge of their language," wrote Lalonde. By contrast, where there was little or no connection to language, the child suicide rate rose to *six* times higher than the national average.

That statistic bears repeating. In First Nations communities where the original language has effectively vanished, six times as many children are killing themselves as in other communities across the country where the kids *are* able to speak their mother tongue. In a country where youth suicide accounts for one-quarter of all suicides, that means hundreds of First Nations children are dying at their own hands every year. The link to a lack of connection to their culture, writes Lalonde, is irrefutable: "Loss of language is the canary in the coalmine of cultural distress."

Renée Sampson, a young SENĆOŦEN language teacher from SELILIYE's community of Tsartlip, is an aunt acutely aware of the importance of this issue to her nieces and nephews: "All our social problems stem from the disconnection of our young people to our culture because they don't know our language," she explains. "Without that sense of cultural identity, they just don't know who they are." Mike Willie, who has worked extensively in the field of cultural preservation and revitalization on northern Vancouver Island in British Columbia, agrees fervently: "If you don't have the language, if you don't know who you are, you're just roaming this world, lost. You're not grounded anywhere."

But the converse, as the Lalonde report so poignantly emphasizes, is also true. Mike was born in 1977 in the remote community of Kingcome Inlet on British Columbia's central coast, and grew up hearing his Musgamakw Dzawada'enuxw language and songs at his Elders' knees. But Kingcome Inlet is isolated, and after Grade 7, families have to send their children away to complete their education. "I was sent to Victoria," he says. "No one there spoke my language, and I really struggled. It was a huge culture shock." Mike believes what saved him was his upbringing, steeped in his mother tongue: "Having been taught in my language as a young child totally helped me survive the experience."

But the language was also far more than a safety blanket to cling to in an alien environment. Mike says it unquestionably helped him do better at school in general: "I have no doubt that knowing the language and the songs helped me with my self-confidence and getting through school and university. That's true of many kids from Kingcome Inlet," he adds. "There is a really high success rate amongst our youth in post-secondary education, and I attribute it directly to being grounded in the language."

People like Mike and Renée, and the children they both work with, are living proof that learning their language pays off for First Nations youth in terms of cultural and general well-being. One Thanksgiving a few years ago, Renée watched her then sixteen-year-old niece lead her cousins in performing a SENĆOŦEN drum song. "I was watching her and the others," she recalls, "and thinking, here are these teenagers—they are at the point where they could be out drinking, dropping out of school, getting pregnant—and they're not! They've embraced the language instead, and they're proud and they're healthy."

The evidence goes well beyond the anecdotal. After decades of research and pilot language programs in various countries, it is now well established that children versed in their mother tongue, as well as the dominant cultural language, do well in all areas of education. Papua New Guinea has provided mother-tongue education to all of its children since 1993. Dr. Andrea Bear Nicholas, former chair of Native Studies at St. Thomas University in Fredericton, New Brunswick, observes: "The results are striking. Children become literate more quickly and learn English faster than children who went through the old unilingual system, and score higher in all subjects. The dropout rate has also decreased."

The same results have emerged in Canada. Tracey Herbert, executive director in 2015 of British Columbia's First Peoples' Cultural Council, notes the success of Mohawk and Cree immersion schools founded in Ontario in the mid-1980s: "Their kids have higher high school graduation rates than national averages, and some of the highest rates of follow-through into post-secondary education of any First Nations in Canada." In British Columbia, the N'kmaplqs i Snma'mayat'tn klSqilxwet (Okanagan Indian Band Cultural Immersion School) is the region's first school with Okanagan language and knowledge as its foundation. Dr. Bill Cohen, a band councillor and former associate professor of Indigenous Studies at Okanagan University College, helped establish the Kindergarten to Grade 7 school in 2008.

"The community has two fundamental goals it wants to achieve with the school," says Dr. Cohen. "They want the kids to be fluent in their language—to speak, think, and dream in it. Equally importantly, they want the children to be successful in the provincial school curriculum and in gaining world knowledge. We're well on the way to meeting both those goals," he adds with satisfaction.

Cohen says that most of the children going through the program shine when they enter the mainstream high school system, getting onto honour rolls, principals' lists, and school sports teams. "There's a real difference in these kids," he observes. "They're more confident in public. They are healthy, happy young people who are succeeding in the public school system with ease." Kathy Michel, cofounder of the Chief Atahm immersion school in Chase in central British Columbia, has had the same experience: "When my children entered the public school system at Grade 11, they opened up their science book and said, 'Oh, this is easy stuff. We were taught this way back in Grade 5.'"

What immense hope these stories signify for every First Nations child in this country, and for Canada. After all, First Nations are the fastest-growing segment of the population. That statistic represents hugely exciting potential for this country. Imagine a Canada where millions of First Nations youth and adults speak their languages every day as well as English or French, and are healthy, happy, and doing well in their lives. Don't these children deserve that chance? Shouldn't we *all* care about that?

If the educational argument alone isn't convincing enough, however, there are other reasons to consider supporting language revitalization efforts in Canada. The moral case certainly isn't difficult to make, especially in the context of reconciliation. We took the language away; shouldn't we give it back? Besides, how can we hope to have a meaningful conversation together about reconciliation held only in English or French?

Scientists have also made a strong environmental case for language preservation, arguing that with the extinction of any Indigenous language, a wealth of knowledge about animals, plants, mathematics, navigation, and medicine is also lost.

Non-Indigenous fisheries scientists insisted for decades, for example, that a particular type of salmon was just one species, despite the fact that First Nations have two different names for it. DNA testing ultimately proved the scientists wrong. This is highly valuable knowledge that we simply cannot afford to throw away.

Active efforts to support First Nations languages come at a cost, of course. But Dr. Peter Heap, a retired government official and former director of the First Peoples' Cultural Foundation, says bluntly it is money immensely well-spent: "The evidence is blindingly strong that a healthy language contributes to a healthy community. An unhealthy one puts a disproportionate burden on the social welfare system. Ultimately, the taxpayer is going to pick up a much bigger tab for that."

Dr. Bear Nicholas agrees, in equally candid terms: "Providing mother-tongue education for First Nations children would avoid the expense involved in addressing high dropout rates, including social and financial costs associated with welfare, addictions, suicide, incarceration and poor health." She cites this compelling example: the cost of a private tutor in a mother-tongue language for nine years is significantly less than keeping someone in prison for just one year.

The cultural and emotional saving is, of course, immeasurable. In 2010, SELILIYE graduated from Grade 12 at LÁU,WELNEW Tribal School, to which she had returned that year at the age of fifty-eight, courageously determined to finish school at last. Once again she is a proud and healthy WSANEC woman speaking her language, sitting at the kitchen table as she once did as a small child listening to her grandmother; this time, her grandchildren are speaking SENĆOŦEN to her. I plan one day to emulate SELILIYE and go to French immersion school, and finally become fluent in a language that I proudly claim as my own.

I hope that the names of the first languages will eventually become as well known to all Canadian schoolchildren, First Nations and non-First Nations, immigrants and settler descendants alike, as the names of the provinces and territories. Perhaps the languages will be thriving strongly once more by then, and we can have a conversation about reconciliation in those languages as well as English and French—a real and meaningful dialogue between all of us, in all of our mother tongues, proud and confident in our respective identities and respectful of each of them.

It would be nice to think that by then, we would no longer need to.

WHITE ABORIGINAL WOMAN

RHONDA KRONYK

F OR MOST OF my life, I took my identity for granted. According to the federal government I am Tsay Keh Dene, from a small band in northern British Columbia. But, like my mother and Grannie, I was raised white and have never fully identified as Aboriginal.

I started questioning my identity in the early 1990s when Grannie applied for her Indian Status and Bill C-31 began to make headlines. Before Bill C-31, a change to a piece of legislation called the Indian Act, a Status woman who married a Non-Status man (even if he was Aboriginal) lost her Status. If a Status woman married a Status man from another band, she lost her membership with her family band and became a member of her husband's band; she could lose that membership if she divorced her husband or he died. It's confusing, right? Basically, the law and practice meant that a woman's status was always tied to the men in her life. Even worse, it made it easier for the government to quietly decrease numbers of Status Indians.

Then, when I was in my early thirties and a single mom, I began college before transferring to university. I saw systemic racism, but didn't have the context to understand it. And, in my ignorance, at the same time as I was becoming increasingly aware of problems for Indigenous peoples in Canada, I was often dismissive of "their" customs. I don't think my dismissiveness came from racism, but I felt a disconnect from Aboriginal traditions I didn't appreciate. I was an outsider to a culture that I'm now legally part of.

I'm a proud Canadian, and my background reflects the plurality of this country. On my father's side, I'm mostly Ukrainian and German with a few other European backgrounds thrown into the mix. On my mother's side, I'm French Canadian, Cree, and Dene, with some way-back Brits starting us off in Canada in the mid-1700s. That is the kind of mixed heritage that makes Canada a special country—we're an amazing, eclectic mix of people from around the planet.

I never thought about any of this or about my Aboriginal heritage until I was a teenager, because ethnicity was never an issue we talked about in my home. I noticed injustices and power imbalances, but I never understood them or what was behind them. I wasn't raised to ask questions, so I never interrogated Canada's role as a peacemaker and defender of human rights at home and abroad. When I saw racism in Canada, I thought they were isolated episodes.

I might not have been so impacted by the changes around me if I hadn't begun to learn about colonialism and identity from an academic perspective. My studies made it easy to see the effects of colonialism in countries such as India, the Philippines, or most of the African continent. I also accepted that colonialism was part of Canada's past, but thought of it as a quieter, more peaceful process than that of other nations. After all, some of my maternal ancestors came to Canada in the 1750s to work for the Hudson's Bay Company, and my father's family was part of the European wave of immigration that happened in the 1800s as the Canadian Pacific Railway "opened" the Prairies for resettlement.

If you're the colonizer, colonialism is about replacing the "uncivilized" with the "civilized." If you are being colonized, it devalues and destroys everything you know. In North America, long-held Indigenous ways of education, religion, land use, social customs, and resource management were attacked. Colonial powers wanted what the land held and decided that "improving" the lives of Indigenous people through assimilation was a good way to reach their goals. That's not much comfort to the colonized.

Colonizing nations thought they had all the answers. Europeans believed they had a superior culture, civilization, and God on their side. They also had immunity to many diseases that wiped out the people they met. They had weapons. And they had superior strength. Those elements allowed Europeans to force their image of civilization on what they saw as an uncivilized land.

I didn't like this colonial story, but it seemed like it was all in the past so I didn't consider its implications. Then Grannie's experience made me more aware of problems that I hadn't fully recognized. She applied for her Status when she was a senior citizen. Many of her family's records had been lost when BC Hydro flooded a large portion of northern British Columbia under Williston Lake. According to a government official, Grannie's mother "didn't exist" because the paperwork was missing. In order to get her Status, Grannie had to prove her mother's existence.

I was incredibly offended for Grannie because someone was actually crass enough to deny her mother's life. As I understood it, the government intentionally kept the Native populations of the Williston Lake area in the dark about their plans to flood their homes and hunting grounds, and so many records were lost. Somehow the lack of records made the government think it was okay to claim that individual people had not lived.

I revisited the WAC Bennett Dam recently. I asked the young man at the information desk a question and was surprised by the answer. When I inquired about the exact locations of the former HBC fort and Indigenous communities, I was informed that there were no settlements in the area when the dam was flooded. BC Hydro has paid millions of dollars in reparations, yet apparently trains its employees to claim that there was no controversy over the dam. Even after she's passed away, they're trying to take Grannie's identity away from her.

After Grannie got her Status, I started to learn more about

her father, William Fox. My great-grandfather published a short account of his family's history in the Prince Rupert, BC, newspaper soon before his death in 1925. That account has made it possible for me to trace his family's movements to the mid-1700s in Moose Factory, James Bay at the south end of Hudson Bay. As I explored the period and the role of the HBC, I began to understand the importance of the Indigenous side of my heritage. My great-grandfather's European ancestors married or co-habitated with Cree women. Some of them embraced the Indigenous life and were accepted by their extended families. One of my Irish ancestors was given the name Fox by the local Cree because he was such a good hunter. That surname survived in my family for many generations.

Clearly there could be a collaborative side to colonialism, like the more positive sounding "contact relations" people learn about in school now. The HBC had a profound effect on Indigenous tribes and vice versa, and at this point I don't think the contact between the HBC and the Cree was all bad. It appears as if both sides benefited from the relationship, if in different ways.

. . .

My exploration of my identity and Canada's past didn't stop with genealogy, though. It expanded when Bill C-31 made it possible for me to get my Status and opened my eyes to the extent of colonialism in modern Canada. Bill C-31 seeks to eliminate some of the gender discrimination embedded in the Indian Act, but it passed only because a Canadian woman took her case to the UN Human Rights Committee. In 1982 the committee ruled that parts of Canada's Indian Act did not comply with the International Covenant on Civil and Political Rights. Yet the Canadian government continued to stall, and the bill did not become law until 1985. The long court battle demonstrates how far the government will go to keep women from maintaining their Status and to limit it to as few Indigenous individuals as possible.

Grannie's experience with the Department of Indian Affairs and my receiving Status under Bill C-31 were separated by many years, but they made me aware of discrimination I had not previously recognized. I didn't use the word "colonialism," but I understood that paternalistic attitudes had been alive and well in successive Canadian governments as they implemented policies about Aboriginal peoples. Now, after years of research into my own family's history and that of our country, I *do* use the word "colonialism."

So what does identity have to do with colonialism? What makes a person Indian/Aboriginal/Indigenous/Métis/Inuit in Canada? Does our identity come from our upbringing, from a personal sense of who we are? Or is it tied to outside sources such as community and government? And does a democratic government have the right to tell us how we should identify ourselves?

None of these questions would be particularly important if Canada had thrown off its colonial legacy generations ago. Unfortunately, we still have to think about colonial policies and the impact they have on identity, because Canada is still a colonial country. Think of recent headlines about missing and murdered Aboriginal women, starvation on Prairie reserves, or sewage problems on many reserves so severe that the Indigenous Canadians there live in worse conditions than people in Third World countries. These are symptoms of a colonial system that isn't working.

Think of land claims negotiations and treaty rights settlements. As a proud Canadian, it makes me sad to see treaties that have been ignored and thrown away by the group with the power to do so. And to realize that treaty negotiations have often been conducted without Aboriginal representatives, or conducted in an unfamiliar language—and sometimes even in bad faith by the English-speaking participants.

Yet for all the deep-rooted problems in our government's relationship with our Indigenous peoples, I continue to have a visceral reaction to the words "colonialism" and "genocide." They're offensive and I don't want to apply them to the country I love. But my feelings can't change reality.

Modern Canada is still a colonial country. Our European ancestors came to this land, took it over politically, socially, culturally, and economically, and settled it at the expense of its Indigenous inhabitants. They occupied land that wasn't theirs and made no reparations for that occupation. Little has changed in the centuries since.

Genocide—another horrible word. But when I learn that Duncan Campbell Scott, the man largely credited with creating the residential school system, said that "our objective is to continue until there is not a single Indian in Canada," and Prime Minister Mackenzie King thought that Canada should "remain a white man's country," what other word should I use? When I see shortages of food, clean drinking water, and medical help on reserves today, what am I to think? Even with people like Grannie and others using Bill C-31 to regain the Status that was stolen from them, Status Indians are going to disappear from Canada because the government works against individuals trying to regain their Indigenous entitlements.

Yet even though "colonialism" and "genocide" are the correct words to use in Canada's modern context, I wonder if they do more harm than good. Do they create an "us versus them" mentality? Do they offend non-Aboriginal people the way they offend me, a white Aboriginal woman? If so, does that cause non-Aboriginal Canadians to feel defensive and less willing to recognize the problems and work towards solutions?

What do we do when the language is correct but flawed? What do we do when the language we choose creates victors and losers?

Sometimes it seems like Canada exists on two sides of a divide. I find myself straddling it and trying to justify each side to the other. Do I support my European heritage and say we can't forever pay for the sins of our ancestors? Or do I support my Aboriginal history and demand that Canada resolve long-standing problems it's continually ignored to the detriment of all Canadians? Do these seemingly opposite viewpoints have to be at odds with each other?

As I learn more, I get angrier. I get disgusted. And I get discouraged. How can this remarkable country be led by a government that doesn't think the deaths of hundreds of Aboriginal women are worthy of investigation even when their communities cry out for help? How can my country allow the vast percentage of the homeless be the people who made it possible for so many of us to make our homes here? How can our prison system be predominantly full of Aboriginal people who make up only a small portion of our population? How can we claim to believe in human rights when we can't even keep our word on treaty settlements? And how can we accept a prime minister who stated in a G20 news conference in 2009 that "we have no history of colonialism" the same prime minister whose government would not sign the United Nations Declaration on the Rights of Indigenous Peoples?

These questions get louder and more insistent as I encounter small and large proofs that we are failing as a nation. The government has made a concerted effort to make racism and colonialism invisible to the average Canadian. We've all heard the talking points: we spend millions on reserves, we know how to help prevent murders of Indigenous women ("it's not a sociological phenomenon"), we spend millions on education, fire safety, medical attention—the list goes on. But regardless of the government's attempts to hide reality, this country cannot afford to treat our Aboriginal citizens like third-class people who need to shut up and take the "handouts" they are given.

And yet, in the midst of this disillusionment, I see hope for our future. I see Aboriginal peoples refusing to let the government silence them any longer. I see Aboriginal women speaking up for themselves and their rights to equality and safety. I see grassroots movements becoming large rallying cries that all Canadians can support in an effort to end colonial attitudes. It took many years for me to recognize the discrimination Canada's Indigenous peoples face, but now that I acknowledge it, I also see ways to move forward in reconciliation rather than recrimination.

Colonialism had a profound impact on the Canadian landscape. Many Canadians, those from the European side of my ancestry, might say it was for the best and that it's time to forget the past and move into the future. But ignoring the past doesn't make it right. Nor does it make the past go away. Rather than ignore the past, maybe it's time to acknowledge it and deal with it in a just manner. Once we do that, we can move forward in a new direction that eliminates all remnants of our colonial past.

Maybe that's too idealistic. After all, Canada's history is deeply rooted in colonialism. But if Grannie can fight for and receive her Status, and a white Aboriginal woman from a small town in central BC can begin to understand the roots of some of Canada's current problems, then surely others can too.

COLONIALISM LIVED

EMMA LAROCQUE

I DON'T REMEMBER WHEN I first heard the words "colonization" or "racism," or when exactly I first began to make a conceptual connection between those words and my experience. But I sure remember my first experience of them. I was eight or nine years old, perhaps younger. I was in a café in a small town in northeastern Alberta, a town we frequented as a family as it was a major meeting place for commercial and community exchanges for Métis and other Native people. I was sitting on one of those 1950s revolving red vinyl stools with metallic edges, sipping pink cream soda and looking at a comic book, waiting for my parents. I heard an odd noise, and saw a quarter rolling right past my little nose. Then I heard awful words drip from some awful place:

"Hey, little squaw, wanna go for a ride?"

I looked up and saw this fat, red-faced white man, sneering at me. I quickly mumbled no and put my nose back in my comic book. Mercifully, he left—perhaps because it was broad daylight in a café full of people. But no one had paid attention. I think back now and shudder with horror at what could have happened to me. At the time I didn't know the word "squaw" and I had no idea what the fat man meant. I just knew instinctively he was disgusting and dangerous.

It was not to be my only encounter with racism (and sexism, but that is another essay). Sadly, it has been a lifelong challenge. I'll begin with just some of my elementary school experiences. The first school I went to at the age of nine was a typical one-room schoolhouse complete with a pot-belly stove and large chalk blackboards. This school housed one (white) teacher and about twenty mostly Métis children, ranging from Grades 1 to 8. My parents were not keen on me going to school but I had staged a sit-down strike at home and howled until my parents relented. I had fallen in love with the idea of school because my older brother had taught me how to read those little Red, Blue and Yellow books. And my mother had instilled a love of learning from her vast storehouse of Cree/Métis knowledge. So I walked into that one-room schoolhouse with confidence and anticipation. In just a few years I was to dread going to any school. Like most children in the country, I learned about Dick, Jane, and Sally, with

Puff and Spot, and Shakespeare and settlers, but nothing good about Big Bear, or Riel, and nothing at all about George Copway or Pauline Johnson, two of the first accomplished Aboriginal writers in Canada, or anything about Pehehsoo or Wesahkehcha (mythical Cree characters). Instead, I read stories about "great explorers" and "heroic settlers" in combat against horrid and inhumane "savages." This cowboy/Indian message was conveyed everywhere—in schools, in stores, in movie houses, and in the comic books most of us grew up reading. We would have seen them on television too if our homes had had electricity.

Indeed, I don't remember learning about Cree people, much less about the Métis. Nor were we allowed to speak Cree/Michif even though most of the school population was Plains Cree Métis. We were strapped if we spoke Cree/Michif or were two minutes late to school—even though we had to walk three kilometres to get to school. Old fan belts from vehicles were used for the strappings. We could also be slapped at whim. I saw many children slapped or strapped or roughed up. I myself was strapped for being two minutes late. The same teacher also slapped me once—in front of my mother no less! What was my crime? It was clinic day when all the children were getting vaccinated and for some reason parents were also invited. We were all to stay outside until our names were called. Being my first year at school, I must have misunderstood because I opened the door, thinking my mom had stayed inside. Just as I opened the door, the teacher, who was right there, backhanded me across the face. I was stung—more so because my mom witnessed him hitting me. Clearly hurt and furious, she swore at the teacher in Cree but he had already shut the door on us. Beyond that she was powerless to do anything. Neither she nor my father could read, write, or speak English. We knew nothing about school boards or complaints processes; that world was entirely foreign and inaccessible to my parents and community. There were no police who would have ever listened.

This was us in the early 1960s, on our lands, where we owned no property and had no access to any established centre of power. I had to endure that teacher for several years, and even though he passed me speedily from grade to grade, and made much of my ability to read and spell (often making fun of my older brother as he placed stars after my name, setting me up for bullying in the playground), I never felt safe or happy around him. I was relieved when we were finally bused to another school.

That was a larger and more modern school. There were more white children but the Métis were still the majority. I was in Grade 4. What I remember most about this school was that we had to exchange Christmas gifts. Names were chosen at random and I remember having to buy a gift for a white boy I knew nothing about, which made me nervous. Then came the dreaded day of the exchange, and when the boy opened his gift from me, it became apparent that whatever I had gotten was incomplete. Actually, I think my father had bought the toy—he did not read and would not have known batteries were not included. He would have bought according to the picture on the box. I also did not understand or see the fine print of instructions. The boy did not make a fuss; it was the teacher who had a tantrum and publicly shamed me. What was so strange about this teacher's behaviour was that she should have known better. She and her family lived just a few miles from my aunt and uncle's place and my uncle did odd jobs for them, like clearing the land that they had mysteriously come to own, land that morally belonged to Native people. It was not as if she was unaware of our socio-economic conditions. Surely she must have known that many Métis parents, though they worked hard on traplines or at waged jobs, could hardly afford toys for their own children, much less Christmas gifts for school! Besides, in those years the Métis celebrated New Year's, not Christmas. Why she made us exchange gifts in a school full of low-income children remains a puzzle to me! What did she think she was teaching us—white Christian generosity?

The following year we were once more moved to a different school, right in the middle of winter term—and again, without any consultation whatsoever with our parents. This time we (me, my younger brother, and a handful of cousins) were bused to a much larger town school whose population was mostly white. It was the same town where that fat man had tossed a quarter at me. Overnight we became a crouching minority. The all-white teachers knew nothing about us or even that we were coming. They were very strict and often disdainful towards Native children, and I remember three teachers who were especially unkind and easily violent towards us. Our Grade 6 teacher in particular seemed to have a great dislike of non-white children. One day he called the names of all the non-white children and had a private chat in the hallway with them. Most of us were Native (Métis, Status Indian, and non-Status, and most of us with Cree and/or Métis cultural backgrounds) but several were Lebanese or Chinese. One by one he went asking each of us how many times a week we bathed! On another occasion he punished a boy from a nearby Cree reserve with one of those classic three-foot rulers. He made the boy bend over a desk and he hit him with this ruler over and over as hard as he could. To this day I can still hear the echo of that ruler as it smacked the boy's buttocks. The rest of us sat frozen and terrified. I have no idea what that boy had done—I just know it broke his spirit that day. And maybe some of our spirits as well.

This school also had Catechism for kids of Roman Catholic faith. It was assumed all Native children were Roman Catholic so we were all forced to attend. I don't remember if the classes were for thirty or sixty minutes, but I do remember every minute was hell. We were made to memorize Latin prayers and to sit perfectly still. The teacher was known for her meanness and her demand of absolute obedience. If we so much as moved our faces one degree from the front, we could expect a hard slap in the face. I learned this on my first or second day of class when I turned to see if my younger brother was there. As I turned my head back, my twelve-year-old face collided with a plump but solid backhand.

Everything about this school felt like a very bad dream. Playgrounds were no easier than classrooms as the white children also taunted me. I was often hurt and humiliated but never told my parents. In fact, until now I have hardly told anyone, and I have rarely written about these particular experiences. In an unexpected way, I was saved from that horrid school by having to be hospitalized in Edmonton. And shortly after my return from the hospital, I was able to leave this school and attend a new one in a new place where I had the great fortune of having my first kind white (Mennonite) teacher. Under his caring guidance through Grades 7 to 9, I regained my love for learning. I also regained my confidence and was able to keep going, making it to high school, then to university.

These were not the residential schools that Canadians are just starting to learn about. These were public schools. In my area Métis children went only to public schools. My parents' generation of Métis never went to residential schools. As a rule most had no schooling at all. Ironically, the fact that Métis had no opportunity until the 1950s to go to any school was probably what saved my generation as far as retaining our cultures and languages. However, it did not save us or protect us from teachers who physically abused us and shamed us for who we were. It did not save us from feeling frightened or inferior. I am not aware of any sexual abuse in these public schools, and we were able to go home at the end of the day, but in every other way, they were just as bad as residential schools.

Recently someone suggested I should write my memoir (a sure indication of aging), and I thought if I told all the stories of all the times I or members of my family, or members of my community, have faced racism (or sexism, or classism, or every other ism), no one would believe me. Especially white Canadian people. The reality is that I can no longer count all the times I have either experienced or observed racism against Aboriginal peoples. Yet at the same time I remember almost every dehumanizing instance of racism directed at me or at my family. Racism is not abstract; it is an experience. Each encounter, each stare seething with stereotypic assumptions, each distrust, each discrimination, each punitive measure taken, each ignorant and insulting tweet posted—they sit like lava in the core of one's being. Experiencing racism to this magnitude is like being branded with a searing iron. It is impossible to forget. And essential to put in perspective.

So how does one survive such an environment of hate (for it is racial hate), disdain, and hostility? A cursory look at statistics on Aboriginal peoples tells us many do not survive such environments. Suicides and homicides, as well as other forms of unnatural death, are extremely high compared to national rates. And for those who survive, such experiences can lead to a variety of difficult directions. At some point in my young life I chose to survive, and for me, survival has meant a lifelong vocation of researching and educating on Native/white relations and their social and political ramifications.

Somewhere in high school I began to fight back intellectually whenever I heard racist remarks, whether made by friends, teachers, taxi drivers, storekeepers, police, priests and Protestant preachers, nuns, nurses, or train conductors (my dad worked on the railroad so our family was often in trains). But it was during my first two years in university that I began to make a connection between racism and historical events in North America. In sociology classes I learned about racism, although it was mostly about slavery and racism in the United States. In my education foundation classes I had an extraordinary professor who encouraged me to read parts of an essay I had written about my community's alienation from school. Well, what a firestorm my class presentation generated. It so happened the father of one of my classmates was the superintendant of the school I was writing about. The classmate jumped up and in a quivering angry voice defended his dad (whom I did not know), the school, the teachers, the town, and basically called me a liar. This was not to be the only time I would encounter such defensive reactions, and it would certainly not be the only time my integrity would be insulted. However, my classmate's reaction only confirmed the chasm of experience between my (Native) world and his (white) world.

This was probably the beginning of my life's work trying to educate Canadians about the ugly nature of racism. Around the same time I read Harold Cardinal's book *The Unjust Society* (1969), a book I could relate to on so many levels. Even though I did not come from a Status or Treaty Indian (now First Nation) or reserve or residential school background, I could of course relate to the racism and colonialism that Cardinal detailed. The attempts to assimilate Status people were very similar to the attempts to deny Métis identity. And in complete contradiction to so-called assimilation policies, the Canadian governments and society were just as determined to segregate the Métis as they were to keep Status people in geographical and social isolation—to keep us in our places. The prejudices, the discrimination, the hostilities, and the diseases that confronted Status peoples were exactly what we were confronted with. And even though we were not legally—and in some respects culturally—"Indians," my generation (and later some of my nieces and nephews) were subjected to much cruelty as well as denigration of our Métis cultures and histories. Every attempt was made to whip us into white English Canadians, yet we were kept marginalized.

If Truth and Reconciliation commissions means anything to white Canadians, there should be commissions on public schools about their falsification of history and ignorance and disdain of Aboriginal cultures, as well as their mistreatment of Native children. Public schools are just as guilty and should be just as liable as residential schools for their abuse of these children and attempted destruction of Indigenous cultures. And there should be commissions on Métis people whose cultures, achievements, massive losses of lands and resources, and suffering have been too long ignored.

It is easy for the majority of Canadians to dismiss Aboriginal accounts of racism. After all, it is part of the profound denial that racism even exists in a "nice" country like Canada. And while some white people have been open to learning the true history of Canada, many continue to believe in white superiority and blame Native peoples for their problems. And even when mainstream media feature racism, they often do so superficially. It was discouraging to read the article on Winnipeg's racism in the February 2015 issue of *Maclean's* magazine, for example. First, it appears that racism is getting worse. Equally troubling, though, it appears as if journalists have not quite gotten the hand-in-glove connection between colonization, white privilege, and racism. It is easy to report on specific incidences of racism, and, of course, these should always be reported. However, it is just as, if not more, crucial to understand how racism is so deeply embedded in Canadian institutions, laws, and practices. How racism is shored up with mythologies of civilization, hard work, fairness and innocence. But the history of Canada is largely the history of the colonization of Native peoples. It is a history of dispossession, rationalization, and control. This means, among other things, that racism against Aboriginal peoples has been so normalized that many non-Native peoples feel entitled to spew hateful slurs, or even to engage in physical (or sexual) assaults against Aboriginal men, women, or children. Racism is so normalized that those who expose it or challenge it are often dismissed, labelled, or psychologized. All these are classic colonizer techniques designed to deny, discredit, and censor.

Many non-Native people also believe that only "rednecks" are overtly racist. But they do not seem to realize the reason these rednecks can spew racial hate is because they live in a colonialist society that has benefited from racism and tolerates this kind of behaviour. In a sense, there is no such thing as individual racism; individuals become racist because they grow up in a racist society. But obviously some hide it better than others, and some are just more plain cruel than others.

If reconciliation is to mean anything, Canadians need to look at the ways that Canada has nurtured racism against Native peoples. This means looking at all the major institutions that make this country run. For example, how does a judge in Winnipeg get away with refusing to look at racism as a major factor in the death of Brian Sinclair, a Native man, in one of Winnipeg's most central hospital ERs? This is a perfect example of systemic racism where at least four or five very powerful systems (Winnipeg Regional Health, the hospital, the unions, lawyers and courts) protected seventeen medical and security staff members from facing legal or medical charges. As far as I know, in the end no one was held accountable for Mr. Sinclair's death because everyone was protected within what one hospital lawyer called "a perfect storm" of events. I have studied this case and I have no hesitation in saying that racism killed Mr. Sinclair. As it has countless numbers of other Native peoples, whether these deaths were caused by sexual predators, police shootings, homicides, suicides, or diseases that come with poverty and inadequate accessibility to first-rate education or medical attention. Racism is lethal and no country with any conscience should ever tolerate it, much less live off its spoils.

I believe Canadians want to be kind. I personally have many beautiful and socially aware friends who are white Canadian and I know they are caring. But kindness, however important, is not enough. And telling stories, though important, is not enough, because when it comes to Aboriginal peoples, many Canadians are more likely to judge than to help. They need to understand why this is so, because this is in stark contrast to how most Canadians respond to international crises. Clearly, some fundamental change in thinking and knowledge about Native/white relations is required. Notions of Europeans bearing fruits of civilization to savages need to be dismantled from our textbooks, popular culture, boardrooms, and courts, and there needs to be an acknowledgment that Indigenous cultures were coherent, cohesive, and purposeful. There needs to be an understanding of how First Nation and Métis and Inuit peoples have lost and continue to lose their lands and resources, and the devastating impact this has had on them. There needs to be an understanding of how racism is instrumental to colonialism. And there needs to be an understanding of how Canadian society has benefited from all this.

There is no peace without justice. And there is no reconciliation without justice and restitution. And there is no justice without righting historical and current wrongs. Canada has a long way to go before we can say with assurance that our country is a just country.

MARKING THE PAGE

LORRI NEILSEN GLENN

There was a time when all the people and all the animals
understood each other and spoke the same language.
—Elder Betsy Anderson, Tadule Lake, Manitoba

SITTING BY THE window overlooking the cold blue of the Atlantic, I watch chickadees and swallows bounce along the surface of the snow in the yard, picking at seeds I threw out before the storm. Oh, to be that nimble.

. . .

I was twelve when I begged for a pair of mukluks, likely a gambit to fit in at a new school. When they weren't on my feet, they were by my bed where I could sink my fingers into the fur and breathe in the smoky tang of the hide. In The Pas, Manitoba, unlike the coast of Nova Scotia, snow came in high drifts and stayed for the winter. The leather soles of the mukluks were as flexible as socks, and I could hop from snowbank to snowbank to get to school, meet my friend at the Cambrian Hotel on Third for a Coke, join crowds at the Trappers' Festival, all with feather-light agility.

Fur-and-hide-wrapped feet were tucked under most desks, as I recall. My mukluks were pristine, so I scuffed them with gravel or dirt wherever I could find it. Miss Barbour was stern: in her British history class I learned a whirl of names and dates that slipped from memory the moment I passed in the test. In English, Mr. Komenda gave us sheets of Latin and Greek roots; our task was to list all the English words deriving from them. Greek: *logos*, meaning "word, study."

I sat at the side of the room, away from the teacher's gaze and in front of the quietest group, dark-haired students who walked across the railway bridge every morning and passed my house along the banks of the Saskatchewan River. I was curious about their stories, not Cromwell's or Queen Elizabeth's. The teacher rarely asked them a question; it was as though they were invisible. They rarely spoke.

In town, they were called nitchies, half-breeds, Indians, squaws. Soon I would know them as Métis and Cree. They might have been members of the Opaskwayak or Norway House Nations. They might have travelled to The Pas so that they, too, could learn names of the kings of England, Latin derivations of *frangere*, meaning "to break, to vanquish."

One of them, Helen Betty Osborne, came from Norway House, a place that figured in my own background, though I was unaware.

Betty attended school—now named for Margaret Barbour, the history teacher—in The Pas. I wonder if she wrote an essay about the British North America Act, or filled in a sheet with language other than Cree. I wonder if she sat at the back.

. . .

In November 1971—after I'd moved to Winnipeg, the mukluks stuffed in a closet, my blithe and carefree youth behind me, my "Canadian" education in place—Betty was abducted walking at night along Third Street near the Cambrian Hotel, stripped and beaten, driven to a spot near Clearwater Lake, beaten again, stabbed over fifty times with a screwdriver, and left dead in the bush, her face smashed beyond recognition. When her body was found, she was wearing only her winter boots.

To identify her, they lifted fingerprints from her schoolbooks.

Latin *videre*, Latin *frangere*, Latin *mort*, Latin *cide*.

. . .

My 1950s-era parents joked that my baby sister, born in northern Alberta, "looked like an Indian."

"The nurse asked me if I'd been fooling around!" my mother would say.

My sister had exotic dark hair and eyes, a warm tan complexion unlike my pale skin. My mother could laugh about it all, of course, secure in her Scottish and Irish background. We were working class, and like families around us, had no extra money, but a line was still drawn. Natives were other people.

. . .

In most prairie schools we attended, my siblings and I had Aboriginal schoolmates. They might have been Plains or Woodland Cree, Slavey, Blackfoot, Dakota, Sarcee, Swampy, Assiniboine. Certainly Métis. Perhaps even Dene who'd moved south.

We also had schoolmates who were of Ukrainian, Icelandic, Scottish, Dutch, English, Chinese, Japanese, Irish, African Canadian, and Polish origin. The Western Canada we knew was a mélange of immigrants, new or generations old.

Non-Indigenous settlers, immigrants, pioneers, a rolling sea. And Natives. Canada is the site of over 300 years of relationships between colonizers and the colonized. When we throw in language, religion, class, greed and power—all the noble and base faces of humanity—what we think will be a melting pot of cultures and ethnicities turns out to be an emulsion, a fragile mixture easy to separate under pressure or heat. No distinction has been more fraught in Canada than who is white and who is not.

Two centuries of colonialist regulation of identity have parsed distinctions among First Nations peoples, European/British, and country born, native English, French Métis, Bois Brûlé, mixed blood, "half-breeds," among other categories. Language, policy, treaties, acts, and laws have distorted—and limited—personal and complex stories of Canadian identity. Early British and European settlers brought more than pianos, silk, rum, hymnbooks and diseases: they brought deeply entrenched systems of ethnocentric hierarchy and regulation to displace and destroy a way of life.

Miss Barbour, as I recall, never spoke of genocide.

● ▪ ●

"I'd guess Cree."

James hands me a feather for our trip across Saskatchewan. My husband and I have returned from a powwow near Big River where the ground shook under the feet of fancy dancers, and the air shimmered with high-pitched voices in song. James, a Cree artist, is not the first person who has commented on my facial features. I tell him the first time I taught in Yellowknife, over thirty years ago, Dene and Métis government workers asked about my ancestry. I tell James I had worn suit jackets and skirts that screamed "southerner" and a pair of low-rise heels that sunk in the muskeg as I carried my carefully collated workshop materials to the cabin for our meetings. Sessions about report and proposal writing. How to avoid bureaucratic jargon and the passive voice in your memos.

In short, I was an offensive idiot.

James, a Rock Cree from Nelson House who survived residential schooling, starts to giggle.

"It's funny?"

"Well, you're not alone."

Besides, it's not about me. Settlers love to make it about them/ourselves.

Yet in the passive voice, something is done to something or someone. "I overtake" is different from "I was overtaken."

*　*　*

James, who was winning his battle with alcohol, died a couple of years later at a fishing camp when he fell off a cliff into the Fraser River.

*　*　*

Images of her appear like a bird in winter.

A girl I'll call Justine had called her father from a campground across the continent, she told me, returned home to sit on the stoop with her mother at summer's end, feeling the chafe of cement against her legs, the dead weight of what she'd thought she'd left: city heat, sirens, her mother's glazed eyes, plans like spoiled fruit. Crushed cigarette butts in a pile at the bottom step.

I sat with her the following spring, her face and arms mottled from fists, a knife, a Bic lighter. Her fingers flicked at the scars absently. Bent over the foolscap she'd found in the trash, she carved words in large round script, the shape of surprise. Eighteen, belly thick, her hair ash blonde and braided, black roots an inch long. One hand moved to the ragged ends of the braid, then to rub the wall of skin between her baby and this world. Across the field, the snow was full of grit, pocked with the remains of chip bags and bent Tim Hortons cups. Beyond, a metal slide and monkey bars on the playground, a sky the colour of pack ice.

Justine and I sat together in a schoolroom that cold spring; she impressed the page until her knuckles were white, asking me to spell "Montreal, amphetamine," smiling as her other hand cupped her belly. Neither of us could see what flickered a year later on the screen: the shrill cherry of the patrol car light, a man emerging from the ambulance with an empty bag, a dark patch of liquid on the sidewalk.

.   .   .

For a time, "Métis" was the term for French-Aboriginal descent, "Anglo-Métis" or "Countryborn" for descendants of English or

Scottish fathers. Now "Métis" alone stands for both. In countless contestable documents relating to Canada's Native population since settlers planted their feet on this land, we see the parsing of status and identity. Who's naming whom? Who is the Other?

You. Me. Her. Him. Where two or more are gathered, we must make comparisons.

We must make one an Other.

Only three generations ago, anthropologists measured the human cranium to make claims about racial differences in intelligence. Around the time my great-grandmother Catherine was alive, geneticists were devoted to creating typologies to classify homo sapiens. Science was in love with classification, and Galileo's creed—*measure what is measurable and make measurable what is not so*—held sway. Race was an idea no one challenged. After all, it was a handy—and often visible—means of categorizing and creating hierarchies, moral, religious, and social, as well as cultural.

You're an Indian. And I am not.

Today, leading geneticists such as Noah Rosenberg and his Stanford colleagues claim up to 95 percent of possible genetic variations exist in any major population group. In other words, we are all mongrels; there is no pure race. If I were to invite a few hundred people to join me at The Forks in Winnipeg, or a school in Cambridge Bay, or a stadium in Dublin, I can be certain most of the possible genetic differences in the world would be represented. Very little genetic difference can be explained by race alone.

Does this mean, strictly speaking, we are all, at some level, Indian, Caucasian, Asian, African? Other? And how can we tell?

If geneticists are right—despite what ancestral records show, despite the observations of friends and others—skin colour, hair texture, shape of lips and nose are unreliable markers of ancestry. Yet, in our day-to-day encounters, we use those markers, most often in less than constructive ways.

Biomedical ethicist Mildred Cho asks, "Why is it that we keep looking at genes and variations and organizing them into categories?" The fields of epidemiology and human geography can make important use of information about global and regional genetic variation, but 500 years of settlement in the "New" World reveal instead the seductive social and political advantages of defining and mapping race.

Geneticists aren't politicians or social engineers, however, and rarely find themselves among the wealthy and powerful who want to maintain cultural difference for their own benefit. Even if Canadian culture resisted categorizing us into race divisions and gradations, those who identify as Aboriginal in Canada are forced to live as Aboriginal in Canada.

In other words, where distinctions of race are concerned, there is still only power.

•   •   •

Outside, the snow swirls and birds dart to and from the feeder. There are fewer of them now, their shapes becoming indistinct against the white. The fact I don't recognize the species and cannot name them doesn't mean they're not out there, like the Justines of the world, trying to survive.

•   •   •

The Greek *hieros* means "sacred"; *arkhes* means "ruler"; the Latin word *contrarotulus* means "copy of a roll" or "record of an account"; *mixtura*, also Latin, can refer to both "blending" and "diluting."

* * *

Three generations back my paternal ancestors were Aboriginal: the census shows Antoine as IND, and Sarah as MET on one record and HALF-BREED on the other. Sarah, according to records, was the daughter of Peter Erasmus, a Dane, and Catherine (Kitty) Budd. My great-great-grandmother Catherine, the daughter of Sarah and Antoine Kennedy, married a French man. My father, Catherine's grandson, married my mother who was a descendant of Scottish and Irish immigrants. Who knows how much of who I am can be explained by that genetic soup?

But I am part of a human chain that loves to make such distinctions. If a person is of mixed blood, their identity is aligned with the less powerful. Obama is considered Black, despite the fact his mother is white. The term Americans used in the days of slavery for someone two generations away from their Black roots is the same word Australians used for Aboriginals: *octaroon*. In Spanish, *morisco, castizo*. Africa, *mulato*. There are further distinctions such as *quintroon* or *mustefino*. Am I an octaroon?

In *A Really Good Brown Girl*, Marilyn Dumont describes the difficulty in answering what should be a simple question for First Nations peoples, but isn't: "Are you a Canadian citizen?"

... and what of the future of my eight-year-old niece, whose mother is Métis but only half as Métis as her grandmother, what will she name herself and will there come a time and can it be measured or predicted when she will stop naming herself and crossing her own mind.

· · ·

We suffer from hardening of the categories. We may avoid words such as "half-breed" and "squaw," but we know racism continues to fester under the surface, especially when it's already deeply embedded.

· · ·

Maclean's reported the following on January 22, 2015: Canada's Aboriginal population has a lower life expectancy than the national average, 2.7 times the dropout rate, 6.1 times the homicide rate, 2.3 times the infant mortality rate, 2.1 times the unemployment rate, and 10 times the incarceration rate. Further, 49 per cent of Canada's Aboriginal population lives in remote communities, and to most Canadians this population is largely invisible.

Meanwhile #1:

A person responsible for educating young people writes on social media:

Oh God, how long are aboriginal people going to use what happened as a crutch to suck more money out of Canadians? ... They have contributed NOTHING to the development of Canada. Just standing with their hand out. Get to work, tear the treaties and shut the FK up already. Why am I on the hook for their cultural support?

Meanwhile #2:
Poet Marilyn Dumont says she can't "unzip" her skin.

It crosses my mind to wonder where we fit in this 'vertical mosaic,' / this colour colony; the urban pariah, the displaced and surrendered . . . are we distinct 'survivors of white noise,' or merely hostages / in the enemy camp . . .

Meanwhile #3:
Theorists sit at a distance, writing about utopian notions such as "post-racial" and "post-identity."

. . .

Latin, *colonus* "settler, farmer", from *colere* "cultivate."

. . .

I am sitting in a restaurant in the small Manitoba town on the Red River where my great-grandmother Catherine married and raised eleven children. It's lunchtime, or, in Prairie-speak, dinner, the main meal of the day. Tucking into their sandwiches and roast beef specials are my sister, my centenarian aunt, and three of her cousins (all in their eighties and all grandchildren of Catherine's). I can't help but wonder how many others in the room are distantly related to me, or to each other.

I read somewhere we mistake the image of our ancestry as a tree; the better metaphor is a trellis. I could as easily share more genes with my elderly second cousin than my sister or my aunt. Or the woman in the kitchen now pulling a basket out of the fryer.

Grey hair, black hair, sparse hair, red hair. Small, medium, large. Around the room I spot customers I'd characterize—if I were asked to—as having Aboriginal descent. This town near the bottom of Lake Winnipeg is, in my mind, the birthplace of western Canada. At one time, fur traders and factors, ministers and merchants married women whose ancestors had been here for generations. It was, as they say, the custom of the country. For a few short decades, this practice was not frowned upon, not tainted with a shame that trailed their descendants. It was a brief, suspended time, when it seemed perhaps the necessities of survival—food, comfort, shelter, and love—might trump the blinkered, acquisitive, dominance-driven instincts of the human animal. It didn't.

. . .

Storms this winter buried the yard in snow, and I no longer see sparrows or swallows. When I throw seeds out the door, the first to reach the food are the crows. The wind creates white-out conditions; it looks a lot like wilderness out there. An easy observation to make from the comfort of the house.

I think of the infinite number of encounters and stories we are made from, the poverty of language to gather them all, and the forces of a culture that render them invisible. The philosopher Emmanuel Levinas pares ethics down to the simplicity and power of a face-to-face encounter: we are responsible to each other.

Who perishes when we don't pay attention? What differences are reinforced when we do? Years ago, I wrote:

> The old country of awareness
> has no record of your name.
> Your name. You would do well to give
> that up, too . . .

A feeble gesture toward abandoning my not-so-invisible cultural backpack, which none of us can do. Meanwhile, the snow falls. As the years pass, we see few changes. We gather statistics and forget numbers are people. Leah Anderson, Felicia Solomon, Tina Fontaine, Helen Betty Osborne and hundreds more populate a wretched graveyard our country fails to acknowledge. We are responsible: We are Indian. We are white.

Perhaps Mr. Komenda taught the Latin phrase *omnibus meis propinquis*. I can't remember. I prefer "'all my relations" or, one I'm trying to learn: *Niw_Hk_M_Kanak*.

LOST FIRES STILL BURN

CARISSA HALTON

MY HUSBAND AND his client, Darren, were walking back to Parkdale School from lunch at the 7-Eleven in Edmonton's inner city when a voice called out from a sagging porch. "Pull up your pants!" the stranger demanded, apparently unprovoked but for a flash of boxer shorts peeking from the teenager's pants. The bull of a man started down the sidewalk towards Mat and Darren, whose braids stretched along his hoodie's strings down to his chest.

Before the man had interrupted, they'd been talking about

Darren's home. Not the group home where he lived with a half dozen other kids but of Home, a four-hour drive away surrounded by bush. Mat listened deeply, like any good "success coach" must. At the time, Alberta had the highest junior high dropout rate of any province in Canada, and many of the kids who quit were wards of the government. Mat's job was to help foster kids stay in school, and he did that partially through advocacy. So when a social worker forgot to think like a parent and moved a child to a different part of the city in the middle of exams due to "bed availability," Mat said, "The kid's writing exams and he's finally bonding to a teacher. Can he at least continue at this school until summer?" Without such support, kids could move schools two, four, eight times in a year. "No wonder they have 'behaviours,'" he'd tell me.

While Mat's client files represented all the cultural groups in the city, a disproportionate number of kids were Aboriginal. In Edmonton, while Aboriginals make up 5 percent of the city's population, Aboriginal children make up 70 percent of the child welfare authority's case files. Like all kids, they felt a sense of loss for their families, but this was compounded by displacement from the band lands where they'd been born. There was something further that eroded their sense of confidence, something a white guy like Mat couldn't put a finger on until one day it erupted like a geyser before him. Racism generally held under the crust of Canadian decorum found a vent in the shape of a thirteen-year-old boy.

"Pull 'em up," the stranger ordered Darren again, then positioned his bulging body toe-to-toe with Darren's lanky one.

Seconds that felt like minutes passed before the spell was broken. "Get a job, you fucking *nitchie*," he said, and spit on Darren's high tops. Darren's fists tensed to rise, then his shoulders shrugged and he raised his hood. For the first time in his adult life Mat was ready to fight a battle he was certain to physically lose, yet Darren walked away.

"How did you not hit him?" Mat asked when he caught up.

"I told you I'm trying to change," Darren said. "It happens every day. I can't fight them all."

* * *

While this is a story of optimism, of change, I must rewind just a little. The hate that Darren faced that day, a block from his junior high, was this same hot, barely hidden racism that inspired so much duplicity in the early years after the treaties were signed. The chiefs of Treaty 6 had negotiated hard for education for their children so they'd be able to make their way in both worlds. Instead of learning, however, their communities were presented with residential schools where children were often forced to board and be taught basic housekeeping and manual labour skills by teachers barely educated themselves. The abuse is well documented, as is the impact on the social fabric of Aboriginal communities.

As residential schools became discredited, though by no means abolished, the welfare system became the agent of assimilation. The Sixties Scoop lasted well into the 1980s, and over that time, 20,000 Aboriginal children were removed from families without consent and quickly adopted out to white families—sometimes as far away as England, Australia, and New Zealand. While social challenges proliferated in the communities most impacted by residential schools (and a myriad of other racist policies that took men's jobs away, band lands away, and women's status away), many children were removed not due to unsafe conditions but due to cultural ignorance. Staff had little understanding of cultural traditions and values. Who knew that a family could share a one-bedroom house and raise functioning members of society? Who trusted that a family could feed their family without an indoor stove? Poverty and cultural practices were, to Western eyes, unacceptable risks. The Sixties Scoop became the world of today, where the number of Aboriginal kids in government care outpaces the height of the residential school population by three to one.

I feel immobilized when I, a product of a hodgepodge of British immigrants who trickled into Canada after the First World War, focus too long on the tragedy of these years. I feel like how I imagine one feels in the path of a breaking dam whose water rushes to surround then drown.

It is the voice of a Cree man who thaws my frozen instincts. He forces my focus away from the flood and towards the surrounding landscape ablaze with sunshine. "There is much loss," the man said. I was interviewing him for an article on decolonization in the justice system and paused as he flattened his hands on the dining table where his three children were similarly taught, "There is much loss—but all is not lost."

.   .   .

Patti Brady is a social worker and deputy executive director at Bent Arrow Traditional Healing Society; she has this spark of quiet optimism too, despite her experience as a child on the inside of a client file. Her mom used to serve her and her siblings "hard-time pancakes" when the pantry and fridge were empty again. These resourceful meals were one of many things she loved about her mom. Outside the dining room window, northern Ontario's boreal forest stretched to Thunder Bay. Their small home was part of the Lake Helen reserve on land belonging to the Red Rock band, where in almost every direction of Patti's home lived an auntie. Whenever Patti's mom was gone for long, the Brady kids traipsed to an auntie's place—until 1962, when Patti's dad moved the family out west. He was a white man and, while he didn't drink like his wife, he was absent and cruel. In Edmonton, the family of ten found shelter in two bare rooms (each contained a bed and counter with a hotplate) in a poorly maintained house where they shared a bathroom with tough-looking strangers.

"The scariest thing for me," remembered Patti, "was we didn't have our aunties." Their dad disappeared to the logging camps and their mom disappeared to drink. Eventually, an official-looking stranger arrived at their door and the woman saw poverty and unsupervised kids. Her file probably mentioned their mother was a drinker, and while for a white woman this might have been improper, for an Aboriginal woman this was a crime. In 1962 it was illegal for Aboriginal people to both drink in bars and buy alcohol in stores. Patti's older siblings assured her, "Everything will be okay. Just go with her and we'll all be home soon." The fair skinned Patti sat alone in the back seat of the stranger's car for the two-and-a-half-hour drive to a cottage at Sylvan Lake where a kind mother, available father, and three young boys vacationed in the summer. The family wanted a daughter.

The social worker left the eight-year-old there with a voucher for clothing and bid farewell without explaining when she might be back.

"Would you like to go see the lake?" her foster mom asked the Ojibway girl.

"No, thank you," she said.

"What would you like to do?" the woman asked.

"I just want to go to bed." It was early afternoon, but something inside the woman told her to give the little girl space, so she stood outside the child's door and listened anxiously to her racking sobs.

In the days and weeks that followed, Patti expected the stranger to come back at any moment to return her to her family, but she also began to settle in. A few months turned into many years. Her mother died and Patti was permanently placed with the family. After being the youngest of eight, she became the oldest in a white, middle-class, Jesus-loving family. Though she was never adopted, she went on trips to Hawaii, summered at the cottage, and followed the foster family's lead. *Just be like them, act like them*, she'd coach herself. *Try your best to be good so you're not given away again.*

Despite trying her hardest to fit in, she did not. "There is something special about the sun," she once said to her foster mom.

The woman let out a peal of friendly laughter. "You're just such a strange little girl," she said.

"No, no," Patti would backtrack, "I'm not." But she knew. She was different.

"There was something big missing in my life," Patti told me over coffee and Portuguese tarts at a bakery halfway between my home and the Bent Arrow offices. We looked out on a busy thoroughfare that, while revitalizing, showed the scars of a difficult few decades. Patti's oldest brother wandered these streets homeless and addicted. He'd tried to make a go of it alone as his siblings woke up in addresses across the city. As each Brady sibling became an adult, they found each other, and Patti learned she was the only one to live with the same foster family until adulthood.

"Despite that my foster family loved and cared for me, I always wanted *my* family," said Patti. "We underestimate the power of connection. I believe in 'blood memory,' a presence in your being that says something in your core is missing, even if you have all these other things that colonization has made you think is necessary to live and adapt to this kind of society."

The racism she faced was more insidious than Darren's. One day Patti and her foster dad met with a school counsellor to develop a plan for graduation. The counsellor asked her, "What do you want to be, Patti?"

"I want to be a nurse," she said.

As they walked out of the school, her foster dad said, "You know you can't do that, right?"

"Well, why not?" Patti asked.

"It's because you're part Native," he said as though this was an obvious fact. "You'd never be able to finish the classes."

It wasn't until after she'd married and raised three children that she went to university. It was there that she learned of the strength of her culture. With some trepidation she went to a pipe ceremony, then with increasing hunger experienced round dances and powwows, smudges and sweats.

· · ·

Despite the fact that over her lifetime she has watched the disproportionate numbers of Aboriginal kids in the foster system grow, Patti believes not only that the system must change, but that it *can* change.

Part of this change is about working differently. But how? When in 2012 Bent Arrow partnered with the provincial government to support Aboriginal families involved with Child and Family Services in Edmonton, Patti and other leaders at Bent Arrow sought the answer to this question by bringing flags and protocol to the Elders. Cheryl Whiskeyjack is CEO of Bent Arrow and an Ojibway from southern Ontario. Over Italian meatballs one block away from Edmonton's Chinatown, she explained to me the vision of the Sundance that they received: "The sundancer puts themselves in a position of sacrifice for four days and four nights. No drinking. No eating. They do sweats and they dance from sun-up to sundown. They pray all the time, focusing entirely on the colourful flags that hang on the Tree of Life at the centre of the circle. The pieces of fabric represent hundreds of different prayers from the people. The sundancer is dancing for each person, that he will get his answer. They are dancing for you, for me, for my grandma. They are doing it for everyone but themselves."

For Bent Arrow it became clear that practising differently meant seeing their families as sundancers. "Our families are putting themselves in a place to change; they are sacrificing things for their children, their families, and their community, and if we treated them as if they were in a position of honour, then the whole way we approach working with them certainly would be different."

Every sundancer also has an *oskapewo*, a sacred helper. The oskapewo makes sure the fire burns; he brings blankets, chops wood, and does whatever the sundancer requires so she can focus on why she's there. "That is our job as practitioners," said Cheryl. "Our job is to support our families—not to tell them what to do but to support the work *they* are doing."

In ceremony, the Elders prayed for a name for the program that would deliver different kind of care. *Kahkiyaw*, it would be called, meaning "All in this together." The following two years they watched the number of children taken into government custody drop from 60 percent of all client files to forty. Cheryl says the success is largely due to more *oskapewis* working with parents, like the time a pregnant woman called Cheryl in a panic.

For two years the Aboriginal woman had worked a low-paying job and stayed clean and sober after years of addiction. When she discovered she was pregnant, she felt great joy and then great fear. This would be her fifth child, but a quiet home greeted her every night she returned from work. She had lost guardianship of her first four children, and despite being clean she knew that if she didn't find help she would lose this baby too. She called Cheryl; she was willing to take classes, to do drug tests, to move—anything, if it meant she could keep her final baby.

The woman gave birth, and when Cheryl arrived at the hospital, Mom's eyes glowed and her baby lay wrapped in a blanket with a tiny knitted toque that covered a shock of black hair. The government caseworker was there too and the three of them discussed "next steps." The caseworker knew the demons Mom battled were difficult ones to overcome. Was it fair to use this tiny baby as a test?

Cheryl knew Mom needed more support, but with help Cheryl believed Mom could do it. Cheryl asked the caseworker to step into the hall. "What is it going to take for you to sleep at night, if you let this baby go home with his mom?"

"If every day I got a report that Mom was still managing."

"Okay, what if we did that for you?" asked Cheryl. "We can check in with her every day."

The caseworker agreed and, over the next two years, Bent Arrow staff visited Mom as she sundanced. She fell a couple times and her support systems were stretched to capacity as she learned how to parent while under a microscope, and while overcoming her past failures. Slowly, the caseworker re-introduced Mom to her other kids. The oldest child was eight and had already been adopted, but the other three were still in foster care. Then Mom regained custody of three of her kids, something virtually unseen in the system as it is managed today.

It happened because of a few simultaneous "miracles." Mom knew someone believed in her. Caseworker trusted Bent Arrow. Cheryl had hope that the system could change. Belief, trust, hope burning like a fire in a peat bog: these core values live underground and invisible until the right stand of trees bring them to life.

There is balance in the partnership between the child welfare authority and Bent Arrow that Cheryl and Patti both respect. The partners often evaluate different sets of risk: the risk of children staying in an unsafe home contrasted with the risks of familial and cultural separation. "You can't expect to heal a lifetime of trauma in three to four months," said Patti of the sometimes-huge expectations the system places on parents, many of whom have had no positive parenting role models in their lives. She acknowledges, however, that there are scenarios where the only safe option for a child is apprehension.

"You can never make someone sundance," Cheryl said when I asked her about cases of parental neglect and abuse. "They have to be ready." So in these instances, Bent Arrow has also challenged the status quo. In 2014, 38 percent of the children on Bent Arrow's caseload who were removed from their homes were placed with extended family through a program called Kinship Care. This program requires Bent Arrow staff to tenaciously search out grandparents and aunties who might ably raise their kin.

Patti Brady can only imagine how different her life might have been had the social worker in 1962 spent time to discover the huge network of family the Brady's had in Ontario. "There isn't enough understanding about the traumatizing effects of removing a child from her family," said Patti. It was at an Indigenous Leadership course for her work at Bent Arrow where she found peace with her past. The students were instructed to make a rattle, and as they stitched the piece closed, the instructor circled the room. The instructor peered at Patti's large cross-stitch, then said thoughtfully, "That is an unusual choice of stitch."

"It was then I realized my rattle represented who I was," Patti told me. "I am a product of two worlds, and the cross-stitch I used showed me that I am connected to—that I fit into—*both* worlds. It said, 'It's okay to be who I am.'"

. . .

Bent Arrow Traditional Healing Society now operates from the red-brick building that once held Parkdale School, where Darren, that baggy-pants-wearing teenager with the braids, successfully graduated from Grade 9. In high school, he and his girlfriend had a baby, and a few years later they had another. These sundancers have created a family and defied their past, all while defining their future their own way. The teens dance with the help of a community of oskapewis, and I'm reminded of Bent Arrow's program, Kahkiyaw—"All in this together."

FROM AHA TO AHO!

ANTOINE MOUNTAIN

RIGHT FROM A very young age I have had a series of "aha moments."

I was born on the land in the winter of 1949, whilst my parents were travelling up in the mountains of the Canadian Arctic, about 160 kilometres north of Radili Ko (Fort Good Hope) in the Northwest Territories. They retained a deep and abiding connection with our First Nations ways.

At the age of seven I was first taken to a residential school in Aklavik, Northwest Territories, several hundred kilometres away, and sent to Inuvik's church-run Grollier Hall two years later. It would become notorious for the large number of sexual crimes committed against the children in the care of the priests and nuns.

My grandmother tried to hold on to me and my sister Judy, but we were sent on a plane anyway—after all, the rest were already there. Then we were separated when we got to the building itself.

Thus began many years of our tight-knit Dene family slowly being pulled apart by colonialist forces we were too young to understand.

Even so, I did well in school and in sports like cross-country ski racing and basketball. But there was always this invisible wall letting us Dene know that we were not to expect anything special in our lives.

One of my first aha moments happened when I was given *The Wind in the Willows* as a prize for some writing I had done. I was always good at writing.

I knew the intent was a good one in the mind of the *mola*, the "white man." But I simply could not relate to this kind of writing, set in Kenneth Grahame's turn-of-the-century pastoral England. That awareness was an awakening of sorts, to at the very least be wary of where I was being blindly led.

At the time, life at residential school was a brutal reality, with its insistence on literally scrubbing the Indian right out of us. This washing out of the natural world we were so used to could only serve to create a neurotic future for us, which it certainly did.

From break of day to day's end we children, some as young as five, were expected to be able to follow orders in a foreign language, and then somehow absorb more instructions in school, with a ruler and hard hairbrush ever ready to mete out harsh punishments for what amounted to our simple confusion.

Some saving graces from all of this rigid new structure in our lives was when our uncle Joe would take me and Judy out on a Sunday. At the very least we could have some traditional Dene food cooked properly by Auntie Edith: rich, fat whitefish compared to the dried up over-baked version we had no choice but to eat at school. We also enjoyed the dog team ride along the east channel of the Duhogah (Mackenzie River), with the snow a faint pink—only possible that far north—the willows flashing their brilliant shades of blues as we sailed by.

It was the same air we breathed at Grollier Hall, only a few miles away, but somehow the freedom that came with it made it sweeter.

Other times that reminded us of our Dene selves were summers at home. People still lived in fish camps along the Duhogah. Life would then follow a familiar pattern, the midnight sun glowing for weeks making for a single drawn-out warmth to thaw cold wintry thoughts.

Yet our childhood games again came to an end when the RCMP boat took us away, and we had to watch as Grandma kept getting smaller, standing forlorn on the shore of the little camp.

Coming up to my sixteenth birthday I was accepted to go to a special residential school, Grandin College, set up to groom a leadership elite for the North. I continued to do well there, granted, but somehow knew that my real life should be back at home.

* * *

Another seminal moment for me happened at the home of a couple in Norman Wells, where some of us would have to stay on our way to and from high school in faraway Fort Smith.

The area administrator and his wife were a cultured European couple, he Jewish, she German. They had two children who lived with them.

From hearing the way they spoke of higher goals and daily matters in an educated way, I knew that I would find something meaningful in their collection of books. I chanced upon Eugene Burdick's *Nina's Book*, which had just been published. With each page of the love and anti-war story set in part at a Nazi concentration camp in World War II, I consciously began to think of myself as a survivor of these residential schools.

In a very real way I was the emotionally dead, affection-starved Nina character, knowing in my soul that there had to be more to life than what I had been dealt so far.

Up to this point, I felt I had been sleepwalking through life, knowing there was something else I needed to do with my future, or at least put into practice what I wanted for my people.

I still wasn't sure exactly what this could be, so when it came time to graduate from high school, I just picked a field and went into Media Arts at Confederation College in Fort William, Ontario (what is now Thunder Bay).

One other student I met there—a mola, a white man called Ted Huff—helped open my mind to all I had missed by being cloistered—smothered, really—in residential schools.

After my first year I worked at a building project in Norman Wells and met a couple of paddling Anglican ministers who needed a guide down the river to Inuvik. They invited me to the first in a long series of Indian Ecumenical Conferences at the Crow Indian Agency near Billings in southeastern Montana. There, near the famous Custer Battlefield, on the shores of the Little Bighorn River, I began to feel the historical difference between the *wasichu*, "white people," and we of the First Nations.

· · ·

We lived in teepees and listened to powwow music every night. I picked up *Bury My Heart at Wounded Knee*, but had to put it back down in sheer disbelief that *this* is what really happened with my people, and why I had been so misled by European education. A few months later I finished the book with the thought that, like it or not, I needed to know my own history.

I already had it in mind to go to work for my Dene people upon my return from studies, so I just walked into the newly formed Indian Brotherhood office in Yellowknife and was hired a couple of weeks later.

Because of my formal training I was appointed head of the radio department. Among other duties, I helped train a number of students for broadcasting. I also hosted the first-ever Native program on CBC North, making it a point to just use our own language and music, this at a colonialist time when even the use of the word "Dene" was a novelty. We also set up the Tree of Peace, a northern branch of the Canadian Indian Friendship Centres.

With the second Indian Ecumenical Conference, this one set on the Morley Indian Reservation, outside of Calgary, Alberta (where they were held for the rest of the seventies), I truly began to understand what it was to be Indian.

To this day, and whenever I am in the area, I go there to the banks of the Bow River, just to relive that soulful smell of sage, with the large camp of teepees all set so splendidly, taking our people back to the days before it all changed. We rode horses, ate buffalo meat, and even set up our own sweat lodge ceremonies. In July 1973 I brought my own teepee and set it up amongst the Nakotas.

These were also the days of Wounded Knee in South Dakota, when a determined First Nations group held the land upon which a ruthless massacre took the lives of hundreds of defenseless Lakota men, women, and children just over eighty years before. We now had a way of making our voices heard with the American Indian Movement.

. . .

Another aha moment for me was the gruesome death of Canadian Indian activist Anna Mae Aquash. In February 1976, her decomposing body was found by a rancher on the northeastern corner of the Pine Ridge Indian Reservation in South Dakota. What struck me, as a visual artist, was that her hands were cut off and sent to an FBI lab in Washington for identification. I did a painting based on that called *Hands of Anna Mae*: they are together, one clenched in protest, the other reaching for freedom.

This was still in my days of drinking and using drugs, though, so life was still in my mind—not all yet in my soul.

After a number of years away, I finally returned home and for a time just lived on the land in my teepee, being Dene. Our residential school years always took us away from home in fall, winter, and spring, when we northern Dene lived a more traditional life, so it took me this long to learn what I needed to do to hunt.

Even today, being a hunter is the real measure of a Dene man, and it was this way I became a contributing member of the tribe. There is indeed no better feeling than returning with a moose or some caribou you know will be celebrated back home.

* * *

When I came to, she was sitting there, a mola—a white woman—calmly reassuring me that all was well.

She told me that I had been in this oxygen tank for the past ten days after being rushed to Stanton Yellowknife General Hospital by ambulance. I vaguely recalled having been on an extended drinking binge, playing some pickup hockey on a cleared rink in Yellowknife Bay, and suddenly not being able to breathe while waiting on a caribou head to cook in a friend's oven.

Now that she had my attention, the nurse told me, "Y'know, Antoine, you are not a bad guy—easy to get along with and able to tell a joke or two. Aside from having survived a serious bout of pneumonia there is actually nothing physically wrong with you. But you do have a serious drinking problem.

"The ambulance got you here in time to save your life. We had to put you on oxygen all this time, y'know. Next time this happens you might not be so lucky.

Now, I am a complete stranger to you—never met you before. If I can tell all of this being here for you, just think what this is doing to your family—your mom and dad, sisters and brothers."

I usually would have said something smart in response, but instead I thought about what this kindly lady was saying to me.

And that was it.

After twenty-three years I have yet to take that first drink on the road back to certain ruin. In all that time I have had plenty of chances to also figure out the cultural gaps that separate us all.

Strangely enough, I started out these troubled times in my life by making a dream finally come true, that of attending art school. The school, called Art's Sake, was an experimental place where we learned the basics of creating art, but no one directed us with a commercial future in mind.

This being the late seventies in Toronto, I became involved with the Nishnawbe Group of Seven, a fluid movement based on First Nations visual principles. While taking part in various shows and exhibitions, I was lucky enough to receive instructions from one of the older artists, who took great pains to let me know that it was okay to set aside all of my European thought patterns to express my own dormant ideas.

A few years later I was married and back home in the North, with one young boy, working with the Band Council to help preserve our Dene culture. I began with the Dene Museum and Library, the first of its kind, putting our history back in order for future generations.

It would still be a decade before I met the lady in the Yellowknife hospital, and my drinking was, if anything, as bad as it would ever get. One day I returned home from another extended booze-filled trip out of town and found our house empty. My wife and two children were gone.

One saving grace was the Great Northern Arts Festival, held every year at Inuvik, where I initially went to residential school. But it was very difficult for me to be creative and paint in a place of such horrors with so many ghosts from the past.

When they finally physically tore the place down some years later, I felt liberated, as if I was now in the present world again, for real. These demons, though, still hosted a downward drink-filled spiral, including a few short months at Lakehead University. My grandparents must have sensed my need for help, because they brought me back home.

Those four years with them were what woke me up, I believe, although physically it would take a few more to put into action in real life.

I did make it a point to spend most of my time on the land, in either a tent or my teepee, just cutting wood to be delivered to the Elders. Even from within the depths of some legal problems, I recalled the words of the great Nez Perce Chief Joseph. As I understood him, the truth is something one has to learn to live with in order to be truly free.

These were times, too, when I would help out on burial detail at home, more often than not for other survivors of the residential schools. I often thought of us survivors of the residential schools as MIA, missing in action, living on borrowed time.

∗　∗　∗

Finally sober, there I stood, rooted in wonder. The ground all around me in a circle about six metres across was lit in a shimmering, silvery aura.

Moments before, I had heard the distant rumblings of deep thunder, *Eedih*, from somewhere farther up the Duhogah. There is a place, across the mouth of the Mountain River, at the San Sault Rapids, where legend has it that our giant culture hero Yamoria chopped open a giant beaver lodge.

I had been at my father's hunting camp at Hume River for a number of days, freshly returned from Lutsel K'e on the other side of the Tu Nedhe (Great Slave Lake), from Yellowknife. I took the time to go out and collect a bunch of vines from crowberry bushes. Our Dene people used these for medicine in the past, and being forever curious I thought to try it for myself sometime.

One of the reasons I now wanted to be at this place upriver from home in Radili Ko was to make a beaded handle for an eagle feather I would leave at my sister Stella's grave. She died some years before, after our rented truck broke down on the way from Norman Wells back to town.

What happened outside the two-story log building began a short time before.

I was just finishing up the last of the beading on the feather offering, when just behind me a sudden sound startled me, causing me to turn from my wooden bench. A strange, small blue bird had somehow flown right through the glass window on the north-facing window without breaking it. It floundered a bit on the cabin floor before hopping towards and flying out the open front door. When I went to look it had made it to some small bushes a few yards away and had taken off again.

Some strange, I thought as I stood in the clearing some distance from the steep banks of the river, where I experienced these wonderful lights all around. Now thinking from the menacing rumblings upriver that something bad might happen, I hurried back in, sat down, and quickly got to the rest of my beading on the eagle feather for my sister's memory. Coming now to the end I thought to burn a bit of the dried crowberry vine leaves for it.

Just as I reached into the pouch to take some out I felt something small and hard in there. Along with this warming sense of happiness, there in my palm was a perfectly round purplish brown stone.

It took a long trip to visit with our Navajo Dineh relatives for me to learn from the Elders what this meant. They said that my sister Stella was so happy wherever she is now that she sent me the nice stone for thinking of her and making the eagle feather offering.

One of the people I got to know quite well in the tourist town of Page, Arizona, was an elderly Navajo man, Frank Tsosie. His English was not all that great, but we got along well and that was good enough for us.

Just then I was getting to learn all about the Native American Church, so we went to a number of the all-night prayer services. At one of these he especially requested the tobacco be sent around the crowded tepee, and in the few words before his prayer I heard him say that he wanted "our visitor here from the Far North to somehow know the Peyote Spirit."

He went into a rather lengthy prayer in his Dineh language, and as he did I had this sense of being taken quietly away, far and up—up a clear mountain stream to a serene secluded spot where everything sparkled in bliss.

In these long moments I did not even dare to breathe so as not to disturb the peace for the ages. When I looked around I could see that my old friend's prayer was over and that the drum was again making its way around, with songs coming from beings that were truly humble in the loving hands of God.

It took me over twenty years of going down to visit amongst our Navajo Dineh, but I am still on my way to express this sense of the ultimate *Aho*.

AHO. Thank you.

A CONVERSATION BETWEEN SHELAGH ROGERS AND THE HONOURABLE JUSTICE MURRAY SINCLAIR

PUBLISHER'S NOTE: The following conversation has largely been transcribed directly from a recorded interview. As a result, the dialogue may at times appear to have copyediting errors. Any such irregularities have been intentionally retained to preserve accuracy.

Shelagh Rogers, INTRO: Hello, I'm Shelagh Rogers. I've been a broadcaster for about 400 years and most of that has been at CBC Radio. I'm also what former prime minister Joe Clark calls an "honoured witness," that is, I'm an honorary witness to the work of the Truth and Reconciliation Commission of Canada (TRC). And it has indeed been a huge honour: it's completely changed my life and my focus as a citizen of Canada. I've met some of the most amazing people I know through the TRC gatherings. I've come to realize that

I make mistakes as I learn about the true history of Canada and I fall on my face. I likely always will, but I have amazing teachers who help me up again. I've also learned through the national events that I've attended—and that has been six out of the seven (I missed the first one in Winnipeg)—I've learned how much I have yet to learn.

I'm very fortunate to have in this singular, life-altering, even cell-altering experience, a very good friend and a very good teacher—a *great* teacher—and that is Murray Sinclair. He is the chair of the Truth and Reconciliation Commission and we share an ancestor from Norway House, a woman named Nahoway, so if you hear in our conversation times when he calls me "cousin," we are very distant cousins, but cousins nonetheless.

I've had the honour of hosting Murray at our home on Gabriola Island. As we record this interview, Murray has been here for just a little over a week. I hope you enjoy our conversation. Thank you for listening. Thank you for reading. Thank you for what you are about to do.

SR: First of all, Murray, I want to say that it's a great honour to have you here at our home and on our deck here in Snuneymuxw First Nation territory. Welcome!

Murray Sinclair: Thank you. I don't know why you think I'm leaving! There's no guarantee of that yet until you actually see me drive away.

SR: This is the guest who came for an afternoon and stayed for eight days. But I'm not counting—I wish you'd stay longer! I think the first thing I would like you to do is to introduce yourself to someone who may never have met you before.

MS: Oh my! I'm so used to being introduced and people doing the public introductions that I'm not sure how to start. If I were to introduce myself to somebody, I would always talk about family. I would say that I am the son of Henry and Florence, the grandson of Catherine and James Sinclair, and I come from the former St. Peter's Indian Reserve as it was called at the time—First Nation, now—that was taken away from our people back in 1907. I grew up in and around that area and went to high school in the town of Selkirk, in Manitoba, and graduated from there and went to university. Graduated from law school in 1979. Started practising law in 1980. Was appointed a judge to the provincial courts of Manitoba in 1988 and then was appointed to the Court of Queen's Bench in Manitoba in 2001, and have been a judge ever since. I'm currently the chair of the Truth and Reconciliation Commission of Canada that's going to end very soon. I'm of Ojibway ancestry but my grandfather's Cree from Norway House. My grandmother, who was probably the most influential person in our family, was of Ojibway and French ancestry from the Manigotagan area in Manitoba, which is right adjacent to the Hollow Water First Nation. I grew up speaking English and French and Ojibway and Cree, my aunties tell me, but by the time I was in high school I'd forgotten how to speak Ojibway and Cree. But it comes back to me relatively quickly when I'm spending time with Elders who speak the language and I can hear it.

I was raised by my grandmother who had been sent to a residential school when she was a little girl—as a Catholic. There's an interesting story about my grandmother's Catholicism that I'll share with you sometime. She wanted me to be a priest and I was a very spiritual guy—still am. When I was a young teenager I decided that being a priest was not for me, and for a while I didn't follow any particular faith teaching but I was still very spiritual. Then, eventually, as a young man I started to explore Aboriginal spirituality and now I'm very much immersed in that.

SR: You have an Ojibway name . . .

MS: My name is Mizanay Gheezhik.

SR: And what does it mean?

MS: Mizanay Gheezhik means "pictures in the sky" or "images in the sky." But as with any Ojibway name, it comes with a teaching and a story. And the story of my name is that it is a name that comes from a time when the Anishnaabe (the Anishnaabe are the Ojibway peoples—it means "human being" in the language) were in one of their troubled periods. There was a young man who was looking for some answers for a particular situation and decided to go and watch the sun rise and see if he could find the answers. The story is that as he sat and watched the sun rise each morning, he would see images in the sky. And things in the sky. Sometimes clouds, sometimes animal spirits that would help him to understand things that he could then use to explain to the people. So the story of the name is that he would then take those understandings back and help people to understand what was going on, or what had happened, or what would or should happen. So the name literally means "images in the sky," but it's translated to me as "the one who speaks of pictures in the sky." So that's how I interpret it and that's what I tell people it means, but it's about that story.

SR: It's a very beautiful name and you are fulfilling the destiny of the name.

MS: One of the teachings about the naming ceremony is that when you are created—the moment you are conceived as a human being—the Creator sends a spirit to be part of your creation. So you have a body, a mind, and a spirit. And the spirit that comes to you already has a name and that name is not known to you until you ask an Elder who has the authority to seek names, until he conducts the proper ceremony or does the proper things to ask the Creator to show him or her what your name is. So that's during the naming ceremony, that's the name that is revealed. So Elders don't make up a name for you, they don't create a name for you, they *find* the name that you already have. Because the

Creator sent that spirit to be with you so the spirit could do its work here on this earth through your body and through your life. So while this being known as Murray Sinclair or [MM] is doing this work, it's actually this spirit's work that I am carrying out. I know that sounds a little bit religious, but the reality is, it's just part of our teaching. So when you come to understand who you are and why you are here, you need to know your spirit name. You need to know the spirit that lives within you, because then that will help you know what your work is.

SR: As you know, I also have an Ojibway name that you gave me at the Northern National Event: Shaganashiquay. And I was so excited I walked around saying it all day long and then I found it means, essentially, "white woman" [laughing].

MS: Well, Shaganash refers to the people who speak that foreign language. So it generally refers to people of European ancestry who come here—and it wasn't an official name ceremony, I want you to know that!

SR: I know! There was no ceremony about it at all!

MS: It may have been hailed across the room at you at the time.

SR: I think that's what happened . . .

MS: It was meant in jest, and in good fun!

SR: I think it surprises people, I know it surprised me at first, to know that through the national meetings, hearing the statements from Survivors about the horror and appalling abuses that happened in residential schools, that there has, in fact, also been humour throughout this process as well.

MS: There has been a balance to the work of the commission that we've always tried to maintain. We knew—and I had known from the beginning because of other work that I had done as a lawyer and a judge—that when you engage with Elders, and you engage with people from the Aboriginal community in a public way, and when you engage with Survivors of residential schools, that the work can become very heavy. The stories are very difficult stories, and the experiences of those who went to the schools was going to be a very emotional experience that we were going to hear about. I had warned the other commissioners ahead of time to be ready for that. But I also knew that no matter what we did, there would always be moments during the day where people would do what they could in order to help us to carry that weight, to carry the burden of those stories forward. And there are always those moments when we could laugh and when we did laugh. I wouldn't say that they were dark humour, and I wouldn't even say they were intended to be funny—it's just that we would always manage to see a funny situation in something and take advantage of that. And it helped us to feel that we were truly sharing in the fullness of everything that they had experienced.

SR: I remember at the Atlantic National Event that there was a Survivor whose sister was in the infirmary at Shubenacadie School. She said, "I prayed to get sick, I prayed to their God and I got measles real bad." And she looked up and said, "Don't ever pray to their God!" And the laughter was just huge. And there have been many, many other moments of that, I guess you would call it, release of laughter. At the Quebec National Event, I remember Elder John Cree of the Mohawk getting up and talking about his name and how confusing that is, and laughing about that, but also stressing that if we don't laugh we would be crying an awful lot more.

MS: We talked to Survivors during the course of the hearings about how did they manage to cope with the things that were going on. Even those who were not physically or sexually abused—and that was a pretty fair number of people—but they were nonetheless in a very stressful situation, in an unimaginably lonely and difficult situation. Some coped with that much better than others. But those who had difficulty coping we would ask, "How did you manage to deal with it and how did you cope with it?" Almost everybody talked about the laughter, that they had to find ways to laugh. They found ways to find humour in situations and I think that's a natural human instinct—it's no different with Aboriginal people as it is with others. But they had to take some very dark experiences and find some humour in it and they managed to do it. Whenever people would tell us their story, there would often be moments when they would tell us about something funny that occurred as well as the darkness.

SR: You provided some of that laughter. I think specifically to the closing event of the Alberta national gathering and you talked about your grandmother and how you were destined to be a priest—that one of the men in your family was going to be a priest, and at one point it was going to be you and went to high school (maybe puberty had something to do with it). Then you wanted to go to university and you had to get your grandmother's signature to get the preparation for the entrance exam. I remember when you quoted her that you were "not to become an educated bum." Tell me what happened when you told her?

MS: First of all, that was back in the days when the education system had a process they called "streaming." So at a certain point you had to make a choice whether to go into university entrance or go into the skills or into the training program. I wanted to go into the university entrance program but they wouldn't let you in unless you got a signature on a piece of paper from one of your legal guardians. And my legal guardians at that point in time were my grandfather and grandmother. Initially I took the form to my grandfather . . . maybe at this time I should tell you the story of their connection because it might help you understand why he said what he'd said.

There are two versions of this story: my grandfather's version and my grandmother's version. I'll tell you my grandfather's version. When my grandfather was a young man he had married a woman from the community of St. Peter's and they had two children. She died shortly after the birth of the second child from a disease—measles, it might have been, or the flu. So he was left as a young father to try to raise these children. He was a working man and he couldn't find a way to do that and he didn't have the family supports in place because originally he was from Norway House and now he was living in St. Peter's. So he went to his church—he was an Anglican—and asked the minister to help him find a family that had a young woman who would marry him. The Anglican minister asked around through the congregation and couldn't find a young woman who would marry a man who already had two children. But I know the Catholic priest and maybe he can ask somebody in his congregation. The Catholic priest didn't know anybody but said to my grandfather, "If you go up to the convent at Fort Alexander where they have a residential school, I'll give you a letter of introduction and you can talk to the mother superior there." Every year they have young women who are graduating that they want to marry off to a Christian because they don't want the children to go home and marry "pagans." So Christian men would go there and offer to marry one of the graduates. My grandfather, armed with this letter, went to the convent and came into a room and was interviewed. He was told he would be allowed to select a young woman from the school so long as he agreed to a number of conditions. All the children had to be raised as Catholics. He also had to agree to convert—which he wouldn't—but they said that wasn't an insurmountable obstacle. They wanted him to convert his existing two children to Catholicism, which he said he couldn't do because they had relatives who would not agree to it. So they said that would be all right. Then he had to agree to send the children back to boarding school and that they would be raised and educated in the Catholic way and become Catholics. He agreed to that. Then, he said, a number of young women were paraded through the room and eventually he picked my grandmother.

My grandmother's version is that he did in fact arrive at the school one day and they could see him. My grandfather was a handsome man. She said she had decided when she had been sent to the school—her father had told her that she was going to be dedicated to the church and become a nun, and she didn't want to do that. By this time she was nineteen years old, which was a relatively old age for a woman not to be married, so she was looking for a way to get out of this commitment to the convent. She says that she told all the young girls who were lined up that day not to agree to marry him—that she was going to marry him. So she said that she had it all set up and that eventually she picked him!

So whichever version you accept, and I always said that I accepted each of them, they had this arranged marriage that seemed to work. They had altogether eleven more children—thirteen in total—plus, of course, our family. So when their children were being born, my aunts and uncles and my dad, they tried to convince one of their children to be dedicated to the church. So when I came along—my mother died when I was a year old, and we were taken to be raised by my grandparents—she found a very willing person in me. From the time I was little, that was the career I knew was mine and that she wanted. And I love my grandmother and would do anything for her, so that was one of the things I knew I was going to do. Until high school when I changed my mind and had to get this form signed.

So I went to my grandfather to ask him and he wouldn't sign it. "You have to get your kokum, your grandmother, to sign it," he said. "I'm not allowed to go there."

I took it to her and she said, "What is this for?" I told her I wanted to go to university and she said, "You don't have to go to university; you're going to the seminary." And I said, "I don't want to be a priest."

That was a very hard time for her, a hard thing for her to hear. There were lots of sad tears that I had made that decision, because I'm sure she had heard it before. She had banked a lot on my doing that. I knew enough to leave her with the paper and not to pursue the conversation anymore with her. But at a certain time the form had to be handed in, so I said to her the day before the deadline, "I have to take that paper back; are you going to sign it for me?" And she said to me, "I'm going to sign it, but you have to promise me you're going to use your education for something. And you're not going to become an educated bum. You're going to do good work with whatever you do."

So I took that commitment very seriously. I always felt—and feel—that I have a responsibility not only to the people that I work for and with—my clients when I was a lawyer, the public in my appointment as a judge—but also to her personally. And I tell my children that when I have a tough decision to make, what would she think if I made it this way or that way? And that helps guide me. It doesn't determine it for me, but it helps guide me to know that this is something that I could defend to her. That's been a stalwart part of my process to this point in time. There have been times when I've been lost, as everybody has been, and have forgotten about that.

SR: Those of us who had been following the national events thought this would be your last address to us, the people who were attending the Truth and Reconciliation Commission events.

MS: I thought it would be too, which is why I told that story.

SR: It's a great story, and very soon afterwards, another beautiful story hooked onto it, where you had a vision of your grandmother and your grandfather. They appeared to you.

MS: I've had a number of conversations with them over the years. But on this particular occasion it was a very troubling time for me because of my decision to practise law or not to practise law. My decision over whether I should even continue to do what I had set out to do in terms of helping people or doing something else or becoming a hermit. It was a difficult time emotionally and spiritually for me, and so with the help of my wife, Animikiquay Katherine, we went to a sweat lodge with an Elder and I didn't know what to expect. It was the very first time I'd gone in one, in fact, but when I was in there I found myself travelling on a road that was a very familiar road to me. It was actually physically the road I grew up living beside. And I was running along this road, and I was running toward something but I wasn't quite sure what it was. I saw the house where I'd grown up, and there standing in the yard were my grandmother and grandfather. They were watching me run and when I stopped and saw them, I immediately went over to them. I thought that this was where I should be and I hugged each of them. When I hugged my grandmother she wouldn't let me go and she said in the language in which she spoke to me that she wanted me to stay there with her, that it was something she'd always wanted. And my grandfather said, "No, Mum, we can't hold him here. We have to let him go, because there are people down the road who are waiting for him and they need him." Because of that she did let me go in this dream or this vision I was having. She had tears in her eyes but she did it in a strong way to let me know that it was okay, it wasn't like I was being ripped from her. In her heart and in my mind at the time, I knew that she was fully supportive of that.

But it was my grandfather who said, "Those people down there are waiting for him and we have to let him go."

It ended when I went back down the road and I could still see them standing together, watching me as I went down the road. And as I got closer I could see all these people there around a fire waiting for me. These were all Anishnaabe people—they were like an extension of my family, I think. It was that which inspired me to believe that this work that I do and have been doing for most of my career was really work that I was supposed to do. That my grandmother wanted me to do it. And my grandfather too.

So I've never hesitated to accept that responsibility. And even in those times where I've stepped back from invitations—I was asked to do this work at the commission twice, and the first time I declined it, not because I didn't think it was good or important or that I shouldn't do it. It was because there were other people who could do it just as well and I wanted them to have that responsibility. But when it came about after the first set of commissioners couldn't make it work and I was asked again, then I knew that it was probably inevitable that I should take it on, and so I did. I have been driven throughout this work and the previous work that I have done with the Aboriginal Justice Inquiry and when I did the baby inquiry, even in my work as a judge each day when I go to court . . . I always think of the fact that these were somebody's children and they deserve at least some understanding of that. That doesn't mean, in the case of people in front of you in court, that they don't get to be held responsible for what they've done, but it means that you always have to give them a chance to live out that life they were given as a child. And try to ensure that they have the opportunity to do it. Because we don't always get that chance. As we learned in the Truth and Reconciliation Commission, so many children lost their lives in the schools at such young ages, and that's the tragedy. The tragedy is when you lose your life at too young an age, or you lost that portion of your life that would have allowed you to live a full life. We have so many out there who have had that taken away from them or denied to them. We need to try to do what we can to help or at least learn from it so that future generations don't have to go through the same sense of loss.

SR: What do you think Canada has lost as a result of this era?

MS: Canada had the potential to be one of the most unique nations in the world with its relationship with Aboriginal people. Initially it was intended to be on a footing of partnership, of solidarity, of moving forward together as the original plan had been. When Confederation occurred, the original peoples of this country didn't oppose it, didn't fight against it. They were prepared to work with it—even those who didn't sign treaties at the time. They had different kinds of relationships that weren't treaty relationships, necessarily, in the same way that we understand them now, but they had alliance relationships. They had friendships that were formed, partnerships that were created—economic, military, and otherwise—that allowed them to believe that they could move forward together with Canada into the future. In western Canada, when the government approached First Nations people, the original peoples—the Métis and First Nations—agreed to certain things that would occur. Agreed that they would share the use of the land and resources, and that there would be no interference with the way that they governed themselves, as had originally been proposed in the Royal Proclamation of 1763. Indigenous leaders knew about that commitment in the proclamation—it had been passed down from generation to generation over all of those years. Yet Canada immediately chose to betray that loyalty, that partnership, that relationship, by trying through legislation (it was basically war through law) to subjugate them, to assimilate them, to wipe them out as a distinct people. And Canada lost out on the opportunity to enjoy that full and equal relationship with people who wanted to have a very significant relationship with them. So the opportunity for our languages to contribute to the language of this country, for our stories and history as Indigenous people to become enmeshed with the stories and the history of this country, so that Canada could talk about its existence from the beginning of time instead of from 1867 . . . Canada lost out on all of that.

People coming to this country now think that before 1867 there was nothing, but in reality there was this rich, vibrant economy, political system, military system in those years and going back to the beginning of time. Understanding of all of that has been lost to the people of Canada. And so those who come here—newcomers—are literally only being given half of what they can be, when they want to be part of this country. Or less than half.

SR: One of your recommendations is to change the oath of citizenship . . .

MS: We believe, as commissioners, very strongly in the idea that we are all treaty people in this country. Because this country was based on treaty and there are many Canadians who don't believe it because they've never been taught it. They think that Aboriginal people were lucky that Europeans came here and saved them from disappearing. The reality, we know, is that Indigenous people have been living in this part of the world for thousands and thousands of years before Europeans arrived. There's lots of evidence, actually, that European nations were in a much less progressive state for a long period of time while Indigenous nations in North, Central, and South America were in a far more advanced stage of civilization. But all of that aside, the people coming to this country need to understand they're coming to a country that has a relationship with the original people in this part of the world—that they are taking on a responsibility for. And that responsibility is to maintain that relationship in a proper way. And what we said in the TRC report is that we need to understand what that relationship was all about. This was not a situation where Aboriginal people came here to

Canada in order to subjugate themselves or to be enmeshed or assimilated into this country. This is a case where people who came here in order to be part of what this country was all about found that they could take advantage of law and other skills that they had to turn the situation around and dominate the original people. And so in many ways—the courts talk about the honour of the Crown—but in many ways the Government of Canada has failed to fulfill the honour of the Crown by failing to respect Aboriginal people. The honour of the Crown is filled when Aboriginal people are respected as peoples. Newcomers, we think, need to be reminded of that from the beginning, by changing the way that we ask them to commit to their membership in this country by acknowledging that they are treaty people as well. We heard immigrants at some of our events say, "When I took my oath of citizenship I did not realize that I was entering into a treaty relationship with First Nations." We need to remind them of that.

SR: At the end of the Ottawa national event when you released the executive summary of the final report, you talked about a mountain. You said, "We have described for you a mountain. We have shown you a path to the top. We call upon you to do the climbing." It's a big mountain.

MS: It's a huge mountain! It's actually a mountain range, probably. As with anything, the moment you get to the top of one, you see that there's another one that you have to climb. But that's the way it is with relationships. Relationships are built on the understanding that each day is the establishment of a new relationship for that day. The fact that you successfully got through your relationship yesterday and made it to the end of the day doesn't mean that tomorrow's guaranteed. So you have to work at it again the next day, and you have to keep working at it.

But in terms of that report and those words that I used, it was really to understand that we have a history that we have to come to terms with, and that's what the mountain is. Coming to terms with that history is important. Once we have come to terms with that history, and reconciled with it, then the relationship will be established. But that relationship, as with all relationships, requires ongoing work and understanding that there will be threats to it, there will be breeches to it, there will be challenges to it, there will be hurdles around it that need to be addressed, need to be overcome in order to maintain it. Because if you don't work at your relationship as a country and as a couple—as people—then the relationship can break down, it can end. You may find yourself at odds again and you don't want that to happen, particularly in a nation where, I think it's fair to say, we all want stability in the way that this country functions in the future. So it's important for each of us to understand our responsibility to make this country function. That includes Aboriginal people, who have a responsibility to make it function too. Once the immediate problems are addressed, and that will take some time, because there's lots of social issues out there that are incredibly difficult to address. But once they begin to get addressed, then we cannot then talk about how to break this country up. It has to be to go back to our original plan, which is to live together, to work together, to make this what it was intended to be: inclusive of all of us.

SR: As I speak to you, we're about a month and a half from when you released the executive summary. There's been marvellous momentum around it—people are reading it, and a lot of your ideas are being picked up by people on Twitter, people are volunteering to read the report on camera so that you can go on YouTube and have the report read to you. There are many other signs of engagement, too. What has this uptake (as we call it these days) meant to you?

MS: It means, I think, that we wrote the report the way it was supposed to be written, and that was to reflect back to Canada what they were saying. We didn't invent these ideas, we didn't create these ideas from nothing. We listened to what people said and we measured them against the vision of Canada we got people to talk about. The vision of Indigenous societies that people spoke to us about. The vision for the future that they wanted to have in this part of the world. And our calls to action were really intended to be a reminder that this is what you want. You want to have a good, healthy relationship among yourselves—Aboriginal and non-Aboriginal people. You want to have a situation in which the things that drive us apart are weaker than the things that pull us together. You want to ensure that your children can grow up side by side and talk to, and about, each other with great respect and mutuality in their view about the future. So here's how to do it.

And so I am satisfied that the report itself has captured the view that Canadians talked to us about: the kind of Canada they wanted to have. And that they're ready for it. They may have been ready for it for a long time. I think some elements of Canadian society have been ready for this kind of report for a long time. Others, perhaps, were not, but now more and more people are ready for it. And there are still dissenting voices out there and I expect that there will be, but, you know, every family has a complainer. And we're going to have complainers too. The reality is, though, that as a country as a whole, where are we going to be, what are we going to do, and be like, in a hundred years? What do we want to be able to say? And I think as Canadians, the one message that we have reminded them of is that all Canadians want to be able to say is "We did wrong, but we dealt with it. We put it in a proper place. We've learned from it. And we've moved on from that and now we're healthier for it." I think that's important.

I really had challenged the commissioners to think about writing a report in which we made no recommendations—that it was simply a statement to all Canadians about what they themselves were saying. And we came close, but I think that there are some concrete ideas in there about next steps because many people would say to us, "I didn't know any of this, and I acknowledge that things are not where they should be, and that we can do better. But what can we do? What should we do?" That was a constant question we got. People were looking for direction, so we tried to give them that. It's not a perfect report—I think things will change, and that better ideas will come along—but for now I think it's pretty good.

SR: Reading the summary is a very good place to start when people say, "What can I do? What should I do?"

MS: I would encourage everybody to read the summary. I think everybody should be aware of the history and there is a very good explanation of the history of residential schools. But there's also an explanation of the history between Aboriginal and non-Aboriginal people, both before and after Confederation, and how that relationship changed and why it changed, and how things came to be the way they are. And that's what people need to understand. When you look around and you see Indigenous people having so many problems both in their communities and in urban areas, you think, *Well, that's because they're inferior people just like we said.* And when you understand the history of this country, you realize that they were driven into positions of inferiority in this country by the laws of Canada and the actions of government, and the actions of society, ultimately, through acts of racism. And so it's addressing those laws, addressing those policies, addressing those actions, and changing them. And addressing racism that we will come to terms with who we are as Canadians.

SR: There's another question I wanted to ask, and this is a quote from Tina Turner: "What's love got to do with it?"

MS: One of the themes of our event was love. We took the seven teachings of many Indigenous societies and love was one of them. I can remember Survivors complaining that we were using love as a theme, because, they would say, there was no love in the residential schools. And I reminded them, actually, that they themselves have told us that it was the love of their friends that got them through it, and it was the love of the family that kept them alive afterward—that got them at least to heal partially from it. And it was the love for their children, and the love for their grandchildren, that is going to carry us forward into the future. Because none of us want to repeat this history. All of us want to have a better relationship for our children and grandchildren, and their children and grandchildren, because we love them. And because we love our children and grandchildren, we need to do things better so that they will be able to have a better relationship as well. It's also because inherently I think that we understand that something wrong has been done here, something wrong was done to very small children, and those wrongs have caused a great harm among a group of very proud peoples. If we love ourselves, no matter what faith teaching you have, then you will feel that sense of obligation to fulfill your commitment to your creator by doing the right thing now. Love is an important component of all that we do and all that we think about this. And in a weird sort of way, those who perpetrated some great abuses thought they were doing things out of love because they followed their faith. And it was through a twisting of their faith that they did what they did. When you feel that it's okay to hit a child because you love them, there's something wrong with that. You shouldn't feel that way.

SR: What do you hope we will be like together in twenty-five or thirty-five years?

MS: That is the perfect point, and a perfectly understandable question. I would say this: that when you think about the future and where we're at today, and ask yourself the question, "Where do we want to be in fifty years or a hundred years from now? What do we want to be able to look back at and see?" I think the answer is the same whether it is on a personal basis or a collective basis. And that is to say that you lived the life that was given to you, to live in the best way that you could. And that you lived in accordance with the teachings of life as you understood them. And that you lived according to the teachings of the Creator that you learned, as you understood them. Because those teachings of faith that we have been given, whether they're Christian teachings or Muslim teachings or Indigenous teachings, they are all about how we must live together, treat each other, and be responsible for the future and to the Creator. They're all consistent in that way. And so in this particular circumstance, on the issue of residential schools, I've always said that the one thing I'd like us to say is that for a certain period of time during the history of this country, this was allowed to happen. And when we realized how wrong it was, and how wrong it had become, we stopped it. We realized what we had done had implications and we fixed those implications, we fixed those legacies, we addressed them. And now we have a better relationship. And because we have a better relationship, that relationship is one that we're committed to maintaining going into the future, and so we have a solid foundation. I think that we all have an obligation to the future, and so it's only when we understand where we come from that we can truly appreciate where we're going.

SR: Thank you—*Miigwetch*—Murray, my cousin.

MS: Thanks, cousin.

PUBLISHER'S NOTE: To read the reports and the summary issued by the Truth and Reconciliation Commission visit nctr.ca/reports.php.

CONTRIBUTORS

CARLEIGH BAKER is a Métis/Icelandic writer who lives in Vancouver, British Columbia. A Journey Prize 2014 nominee and past winner of *subTerrain*'s Lush Triumphant award for fiction, her work has also appeared in *Ricepaper* and *Joyland*. She writes book reviews for *EVENT*, *The Malahat Review*, and the *Globe and Mail*. carleighbaker.com @carleighbaker

TWYLA CAMPBELL is a CBC food critic and freelance writer who has published in many northern and national magazines. Twyla has been travelling the Arctic for over a decade interviewing

Elders and researching relocation and abuse claims. She currently lives in Sherwood Park, Alberta. weirdwildandwonderful.ca @wanderwoman10

STEVEN COOPER is a partner in the Alberta law firm Ahlstrom, Wright, Oliver & Cooper LLP. He was raised in the Northwest Territories and Nunavut where he still spends much of his professional life. His career has focused on working with Indigenous peoples and, in that capacity, he was one of the negotiators of the historic 2005 PanCanadian residential school settlement and is counsel in the residential school survivors class-action in Newfoundland and Labrador. A six-term chairperson of the International Bar Association Indigenous Peoples Committee, he is involved in international law projects working with Indigenous peoples in countries as diverse as Colombia and Ireland. awoc.ca @AWOClaw

KATHERIN EDWARDS, a graduate of the Universities of Victoria and British Columbia, is a prize-winning poet and writer of creative nonfiction and short fiction. Her work has been published in *The Malahat Review, The New Quarterly*, and *Arc Poetry Magazine*. She is a contributor to a collaborative mystery novel called *At the Edge* and is currently working on rewrites for her novel *Faster Horses*. She works as a floral designer and gardener and calls Kamloops, British Columbia, home. katherinedwards.com

CARISSA HALTON is a writer based in Edmonton, Alberta. Her features on topics ranging from social issues to business interests to design have appeared in *Eighteen Bridges, Alberta Views, Alberta Venture* and the *Globe and Mail*. She is also a regular contributor to the *Edmonton Journal*. Currently, Carissa is finishing a book of essays on raising a family in her revitalizing, inner-city neighbourhood, Alberta Avenue, where she lives with her husband and three children. @carissahalton

DONNA KANE's poems, short fiction, reviews, and essays have been published widely in journals such as *The Walrus, The Fiddlehead*, and *The Malahat Review*, as well as in several anthologies, most recently in *Make It True: Poetry from Cascadia* (2015), *Best Canadian Poetry in English 2013* and *I Found It at the Movies: An Anthology of Film Poems* (2014). She has published two books of poetry, both finalists for the ReLit Award, and her work has been featured on CBC and on Garrison Keillor's *The Writer's Almanac*. donnakane.com

RHONDA KRONYK lives in Treaty 6 Territory in Edmonton, Alberta. She is a historian, writer, and editor who is researching the intersections of her family's settler and Aboriginal histories with the Hudson's Bay Company, as well as the ways in which the company created and altered relationships with Indigenous peoples. rhondakronyk.ca @pro_editor

ZACHARIAS KUNUK is an award-winning producer and director at Kingullit Productions Inc., who co-founded the first Inuit film production company in Canada (Igloolik Isuma Productions), and created the first feature-length film in Inuktitut, *Atanarjuat*

(The Fast Runner) in 2001. Since then he has created a number of television shows, documentaries, and movies, and has been involved with the TRC-Virtual Quilt (Nipiqaqtugut Sanaugatigut), an initiative headed by the Paukuutit Inuit Women of Canada to commemorate Inuit experiences of residential schools. Kunuk is also the co-founder along with Ian Mauro of the Inuit Knowledge and Climate Change Project, and was made an Officer of the Order of Canada in 2005. He lives in Igloolik, Northwest Territories.

EMMA LAROCQUE, PHD, is a scholar, author, poet and professor in the Department of Native Studies at the University of Manitoba. Her prolific career includes numerous publications in areas of colonization, racism, violence against women, and First Nation and Métis literatures and identities. Her poems are widely anthologized in prestigious collections and journals. She has been recognized as an outstanding teacher and scholar, and in 2005 Dr. LaRocque received the National Aboriginal Achievement Award. She is author of *When the Other Is Me: Native Resistance Discourse 1850–1990* (2010), which won the Alexander Kennedy Isbister Award for Non-Fiction, and *Defeathering the Indian* (1975). LaRocque is Cree-speaking Métis originally from northeast Alberta.

ERIKA LUCKERT is a writer and photographer from Edmonton, Alberta. Her poetry and essays have been published in numerous magazines and anthologies both nationally and internationally, including *Glass Buffalo*, *The Prairie Journal*, and *The Belleville Park Pages*. She was a writer/researcher in residence at Westglen School and was recently nominated for the Canadian National Magazine Award in Poetry. Erika is currently completing an MFA in poetry at Columbia University in New York, where she is also the web editor for their literary journal. erikaluckert.com @erikaluckert

ANTOINE MOUNTAIN has been a full-time visual artist for over three decades. Originally from the northern Dene Nation, he is now working on a memoir based on his experiences in residential schools and afterwards. His immediate plans also include PHD studies at Trent University in Peterborough, Ontario, beginning in September 2015. Examples of Antoine's paintings and murals can be viewed on his website at amountainarts.com.

LORRI NEILSEN GLENN is an ethnographer, poet, and essayist and the author and editor of thirteen books. An award-winning writer, teacher, and researcher, she was Poet Laureate of Halifax from 2005 to 2009. Raised in the Canadian West, she's currently working on a book about her great-grandmother and other mixed-blood women of nineteenth century Red River Colony, to be published by Wolsak and Wynn in 2017. lorrineilsenglenn.com @neilsenglenn

KATHERINE PALMER GORDON is a French/English expatriate Kiwi Canadian and formerly a corporate lawyer. When she moved to British Columbia in 1999 she was appointed a chief treaty negotiator for the province. Since moving to Gabriola Island in 2003 she continues to work with First Nations on strategic and policy issues. She is also an award-winning journalist and the best-selling author of six non-fiction books, most recently *We Are Born with the Songs Inside Us: Lives and Stories of First Nations People in British Columbia* (Harbour, 2013). http://artsgabriola.ca/katherine-gordon/ @KPalmerGordon

SHELAGH ROGERS, OC A CBC Radio journalist and mental health advocate, Shelagh is Chancellor of the University of Victoria. She co-edited *Speaking My Truth: Reflections on Reconciliation and Residential School* and *Reconciliation and the Way Forward*. In 2011, she was inducted as an Honorary Witness for the Truth and Reconciliation Commission.

Manitoba's first Aboriginal judge, the honourable JUSTICE MURRAY SINCLAIR was Chair of the Truth and Reconciliation Commission of Canada, and Co-Commissioner of Manitoba's Aboriginal Justice Inquiry. In 2000, he completed the report of the Pediatric Cardiac Surgery Inquest. He has received a National Aboriginal Achievement Award, among many other awards, and holds numerous honorary degrees. The Macdonald-Laurier Institute named him 2015's Policy Maker of the Year.

CAROL SHABEN, an award-winning author based in Vancouver, British Columbia, is the recipient of two National Magazine Awards, including a gold medal for Investigative Journalism. Her first book, *Into the Abyss*, has become a Canadian bestseller and been published internationally. It was recently optioned for film. carolshaben.com @carolshaben

JOANNA STREETLY is the author of *Silent Inlet, Salt in Our Blood* and *Paddling Through Time—a Sea Kayaking Journey in Clayoquot Sound*. Her most recent publication is *This Dark*, a volume of illustrated poetry. Her essays and other literary works have been published in a variety of anthologies and she is past editor of *The Sound Magazine*. For more than twenty years she has lived on a float house in Clayoquot Sound in British Columbia. joannastreetly.com @JoannaStreetly

KAMALA TODD is Métis-Cree and has an MA in geography from the University of British Columbia. She is a mother, film-maker, writer, and community planner who strives to facilitate greater understanding of the important histories, perspectives, contributions, and rights of Aboriginal peoples. She runs Indigenous City Media, her story-driven cultural enterprise. Her film credits include *Indigenous Plant Diva, Cedar and Bamboo*, and *Sharing Our Stories: The Vancouver Dialogues Project*. Kamala is currently working with the University of Victoria's Indigenous Law Research Unit to create short videos about Indigenous law. indigenouscitymedia.com @KamJasTodd

DANIELLE METCALFE-CHENAIL is Edmonton's Historian Laureate, author of *Polar Winds* and *For the Love of Flying*, and an occasional columnist for CBC Radio Active. She is a founding member of Reconciliation in Solidarity Edmonton and is currently researching and writing about the complex history and legacy of the Charles Camsell Indian Hospital in that city. daniellemc.com @danicanuck